On Your Way to Writing

On Your Way to Writing

A Writing Workshop for Intermediate Learners

Rhona B. Genzel
ROCHESTER INSTITUTE OF TECHNOLOGY

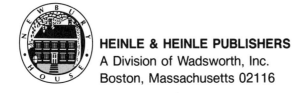

HEINLE & HEINLE PUBLISHERS
A Division of Wadsworth, Inc.
Boston, Massachusetts 02116

This book is dedicated to my family:
nothing is more important.

Publisher: Stanley J. Galek
Editor: Erik Gundersen
Associate Editor: Lynne Telson Barsky
Project Management: Hockett Editorial Service
Editorial Production Manager: Elizabeth Holthaus
Production Editor: Kristin M. Thalheimer
Manufacturing Coordinator: Jerry Christopher
Interior Design: Rita Naughton
Photos (by page number): **1**—Owen Franken/Stock Boston **9, 31, 57, 73, 175**—Michael Lajole; **17 (top), 18 (top, middle), 19 (bottom), 22 (top), 23, 26, 27**—Sue Weisler/RIT Communications; **17 (bottom), 18 (bottom), 21 (top), 22 (bottom)**—Bruce Wang/RIT Communications; **21 (bottom)**—RIT Communications; **76**—Mitch Mandel/Rodale Press, Inc.; **91**—NYT Pictures; **99–100**—Burr Lewis, Reed Hoffman, Jim Laragy/Gannett Roch Newspapers; **109**—Eric Liebowitz; **131**—Boston Children's Theatre; **143**—Peter Southwick/Stock Boston; **163**—Roy Bishop/Stock Boston; **191**—Laimute E. Druskis/Stock Boston
Cover Design: Robert Pehlke
Interior Illustrations: Daniele Erville

On Your Way to Writing: A Writing Workshop for Intermediate Learners

Heinle & Heinle Publishers is a division of Wadsworth, Inc.

Manufactured in the United States of America

Library of Congress Cataloging-in-Publication Data

Genzel, Rhona B.
On your way to writing / Rhona Genzel.
p. cm.
ISBN 0-8384-3432-0
1. English language—Rhetoric. I. Title.
PE1408.G47 1992
808′.042—dc20 91-48058
CIP

10 9 8 7 6 5 4 3 2 1

Contents

To the Teacher

I wrote *ON YOUR WAY TO WRITING* to take advantage of the intelligence and creativity of our students. In this book, students use their imagination, creativity, and artistic talents as they discover what it takes to describe events, write dialogues, fairy tales, and parodies, create letters, and write reviews of movies, restaurants, and television shows.

Writing should be enjoyable, and students find it enjoyable when they are working on interesting and challenging tasks. Students become actively involved when they find the work they are doing meaningful, interesting, and practical. *ON YOUR WAY TO WRITING* was written with these thoughts in mind.

Each chapter uses a novel way to teach the important concepts students will need to be successful throughout the composition process. For example, the introduction uses students' perception of drawings to demonstrate the importance of clarity, background, and knowledge of the audience. From chapter 1, where the focus is on the sentence, to chapter 11, where the focus is on editing writing for a class magazine, students are using creativity and imagination while doing real-world writing.

Many writing books do not deal with the problems associated with word forms and word choice. As a result, students make errors at the word level without any awareness of the problem. A major goal in the early chapters of *ON YOUR WAY TO WRITING* is to help students isolate and correct these kinds of errors.

By far, however, the strength of the book is not so much the technical information that students learn about the writing process, but the workshop atmosphere that creates opportunities for collaborative learning. This, coupled with high-interest-level material, motivates students to write and to enjoy writing.

In addition to the projects and exercises in the book, I strongly recommend that students be instructed to keep a journal in which they correspond with you. The purpose of this journal is for them to tell you how they feel about the class each day. It gives them an opportunity to tell you what they like, what they dislike, what they understand, and what they don't understand. By having students explain what they have learned in the class, you can discover whether or not they understand the concepts taught.

Journal writing is effective for two major reasons. First, since this type of writing focuses on fluency and personal expression, students always have something to write about. Second, journal writing can also be used to identify language concerns and troublespots which need further review. In its finest form, journal writing can become an active dialogue between teacher and student that permits you both to learn more about your students' lives and to individualize their language instruction.

A chapter-by-chapter description of the writing projects in this text is provided below. Included are some suggestions for teaching, ways to supplement the material, and ideas for modifying your role from that of instructor to that of facilitator.

Chapter-by-Chapter Notes

INTRODUCTION

The purpose of the introduction is to get students to understand from personal experience, the importance of audience. For example, the word ***mym***, which students are asked to pronounce only to discover that it is a Russian word that is pronounced *toot*, serves to prove that two people looking at the same thing can see two different things.

The same is true of the picture that includes the word *fly*, which becomes visible depending upon the viewer's perspective. Again, this shows students the importance of paying attention to audience and how much the audience knows. Get students to discuss situations in which they have had misunderstandings, and ask them why misunderstandings have taken place.

Do the same with the smokestack drawing. Focus on the role that the background plays in this drawing and emphasize the fact that the artist's failure to delineate the background is what confuses the reader. Explain that the same thing happens in writing when the writer gives too much or too little background information. Ask students if they have ever been given directions by someone who either gave them too many details or not enough. Ask what happened.

Explain that the importance of background information in writing is to prepare the reader for the information that will follow. The writer must be careful not to give so much information that the reader is confused or so little that the reader can't understand the point.

Once this has been established, move on to a discussion of the differences between writing and speaking. Talk about how tone of voice, gestures, and other types of body language give the speaker and the listener clues about meaning.

It has been said that most communication comes from body language. Discuss with your students how this is possible. Ask in what ways body language communicates more powerfully than words. Ask if they can think of times when the same words had different meanings or connotations depending upon how they were spoken. You can use the following as an example.

(By using the appropriate inflection, students will immediately see the different meanings for the word "no" in this conversation.)

John asked Mary to marry him. She said, "*no.*"
He said, "No?"
Mary said, "No!"

Discuss the *summary of the differences between writing and speaking*, and have students compare the list they generated with the list that is in the book. Discuss each of the differences. Ask students which they think is more difficult (speaking or writing), and ask them to explain why they feel that way.

CHAPTER 1

It seems that most writing books pay little attention to writing at the sentence level. That seems to be reserved for grammar books. Sometimes they, too, do not focus on the integrity of the sentence but rather on a particular aspect of the sentence, such as subject-verb agreement or tense.

In chapter 1, students look at the sentence in its three basic forms: simple, compound, and complex. Students examine the captions under photographs and discuss their relationship to the photographs. They talk about the form of the sentence. Supplement the photographs in the book with others, and have students bring in pictures with captions from magazines and newspapers.

Next, have students look at pictures and write their own captions. You can bring in additional pictures, and depending upon how much work they need in this area, you can spend more or less time having them write captions. Of course, the more interesting the pictures, the more challenged the students are going to be. In addition, you can tell students to write humorous captions, informational captions, sad captions, etc. This introduces the important concept of tone in a simple and easy way.

This work is followed by having students learn compound and complex sentences. You can continue to bring pictures to class for students to write captions. When choosing pictures for simple sentences, be sure the pictures are relatively simple. Interpret the pictures yourself, and write some sample sentences to make sure that your students won't have difficulty with the pictures that you have chosen.

When choosing pictures for compound and complex sentences, try to select more complicated pictures with two subjects and two actions. These will encourage students to write sentences that have two different subjects and two different verbs. Again, write some sample captions of your own to be sure that the pictures will be successful.

Another way to generate writing at the sentence level is to ask students to write fortunes for fortune cookies. It might be fun to bring in a bag of fortune cookies and have students read their fortunes. Once that has been done, you can write some fortunes as a class before having students write some of their own. This last step becomes more fun when students are asked to select two of the fortunes they have written to put into a class grab bag. Reading the fortunes students choose can be quite entertaining.

To continue with sentence practice and to take advantage of students' creative abilities, have students write their own Murphy's laws. All students have had experiences in which things have turned out differently than expected. Ask them to share some of their experiences. Then have the class write some Murphy's laws. These class-generated laws can help to inspire students to come up with some of their own.

CHAPTER 2

In chapter 2, the sentence goes under the microscope, and students look at the word level. They learn to use word order and suffixes to identify parts of speech. In addition to using exercises in which they substitute different nouns, adjectives, or verbs in the chapter to see how meaning and tone change, you can take paragraphs from books and ask students to change the nouns, verbs, or adjectives in order to have more practice. They will soon see what interesting paragraphs they can create by changing a few words. Always work with a given paragraph yourself before giving it to students to do.

It is also helpful to have students underline a particular part of speech in newspaper and magazine articles. Point out to students that they don't always need to know what the word means in order to identify what part of speech it is.

Once you have taught the various parts of speech, as an additional exercise, you can have students write *cinquains*. A *cinquain* is a poem of few words that uses different parts of speech to create its message and its impact.

Steps: Write a one-word title (a noun)
Write two words that describe the title
Write three action-related words
Write four words that express feelings
Restate the title

CHAPTER 3

Writing succinctly is difficult for many students, especially those who come from countries where that is not a virtue. One way to get students to focus on the main idea of a composition is to have them write headlines for newspaper articles. Headlines cannot have more than seven words, and they must express in those seven words the gist of the article.

Using the rules for writing headlines as parameters makes focusing on the main idea more palatable to some students. This approach provides an absolute limit to the number of words and forces students to work toward being concise.

The work in the text can be supplemented with articles you select from newspapers. You can remove the headlines from the articles you bring to class and ask the students to write new ones. Or you can write several headlines of your own and ask students to select the one they like best and to explain why.

CHAPTER 4

In chapter 4, students learn to write instructions. First they read instructions that are accompanied by drawings. Then they answer comprehension questions. Discuss with students what they needed to know in order to complete the tasks. Was there anything that could have been omitted?

Discuss the drawings and how important they were in helping the reader follow the instructions. Then do some hands-on activities with the class so students can watch someone following directions.

Good activities to have students do are covering a textbook, tying a bow, tying a tie, drawing a picture of something, or making popcorn, scrambled eggs, or French toast (if you have the equipment).

Have one student in the class tell another student what to do. Be sure the student following the instructions does exactly what he or she has been told. This is necessary so that students can see what happens when their instructions aren't clear.

If possible, take photographs of each step. (A Polaroid will give instant feedback; other types of cameras will give you material to use in the next class.) The pictures can then be used for sequencing exercises and for talking about both unnecessary and pertinent information. For example, you can ask students to choose the four photographs that are the most important. Naturally, the photos will also elicit conversation and reactions to the activity.

Once these activities have been tried, ask students to select a process for which they can write instructions. Before asking them to write their instructions, have them sketch the various steps involved in the process they intend to describe. Let them share their sketches with other students to get input.

Next, have students write captions for each of their drawings. Tell them to limit the number of drawings to no more than six or four depending on how many drawings students have done. The idea is to teach them to set limits and learn to make choices.

Encourage the use of active verbs, colorful adjectives, and the command form. To do this, choose one or two topics that students have chosen, and ask the class to think of some of the verbs or action words that could be used for each topic. Do the same for adjectives. Have students work in pairs or small groups helping each other identify colorful verbs.

Then review the command form of verbs and how it is used. Ask students what kinds of things they will be telling the person following their instructions to do. Use the command form as you speak about the instructions. Then tell students to write their instructions using the command form.

CHAPTER 5

In chapter 5, students write descriptions. Writing descriptions encourages students to use precise and concrete language. It forces them to help the audience see, hear, smell, and taste what is being described.

Included in this chapter are six photographs of the activities surrounding the demolition of a building in Rochester, New York. Have students discuss the people, the weather, the location, and the event itself. Ask them what they think people are saying. Ask what they think it sounded like when the explosion occurred. Ask how people reacted to the explosion, and ask what sounds people might have made.

Generate a list of words on the blackboard to describe sight, sound, smell, taste, and touch.

Teach the idea of onomatopoeia—that words sometimes sound like what they are describing. People *shiver*, for instance. See if students can come up with other words that are examples of onomatopoeia.

Talk about alliteration. Explain that alliteration is the use of the same letter or sound to begin several words in order to make the phrase sound like what is being described. For example, in "The Raven" by Edgar Allen Poe, the words "While I nodded nearly napping" imitate the idea of napping. We can feel our heads bobbing back and forth like someone having a difficult time trying to stay awake. The repeated use of the letter "n" makes us feel sleepy.

Ask students to find examples of alliteration in the newspaper article that describes the demolition.

Also teach the concept of simile, which is using "like" or "as" to compare something to something else. Generate a list of ideas about the demolition photos from the students.

How much you do with the students will, of course, depend on their ability with the language.

CHAPTER 6

Most books about writing don't deal with writing dialogue at all, yet this is another wonderful way to get students to focus on writing at the sentence level.

In this chapter, students read a radio play. They learn about the directions for sounds to accompany the story, which helps them appreciate the importance of atmosphere. Students can act out the play, and someone can be assigned to handle the sound effects.

After reading and discussing the play, ask students to think of an important conversation that they have had with someone and to write it as they remember it.

From writing dialogues, the students move on to learning how to use quotations. Students learn how to incorporate quoted material into their writing through the use of quotation marks.

One interesting project is to have students brainstorm a variety of situations for which they can write dialogues. Choose one or two dialogues, and have students ad lib them in front of the class. Then ask students to write the dialogue.

CHAPTER 7

In this chapter, students read and discuss the fairy tale "Little Red Riding Hood" in preparation for retelling a fairy tale that they remember from childhood. Encourage them to share out loud some of the tales of their country. Then ask them to illustrate some of the special scenes in their tale. Have them write captions for their illustrations, put them in the best possible order, and write the folk tale.

To assist with this process, bring in books of fairy tales. Spend time reading some of the tales, looking at the pictures, and determining why the author chose to illustrate these particular scenes. Discuss the characters, the plot, or the setting, and the moral (if there is one).

The second part of this chapter involves taking the fairy tale students have written and updating it to modern times. To this end, students read James Thurber's parody of "Little Red Riding Hood" entitled "The Little Girl and the Wolf."

To be sure students understand the concept of parody, choose some simple things that they can parody. Ask them if they know any old popular songs that others have parodied by adding new lyrics. Ask students to share them with you. If you have any records or tapes that use parody, bring them in so students can hear them.

CHAPTER 8

In chapter 8, students learn the art of criticism. This chapter is important for students who come from countries where it is considered rude to give direct criticism. One way to help them feel comfortable with this type of assignment is to tell students that you know that this is not polite in some cultures. Explain that Americans are very direct when critiquing movies, television shows, restaurants, books, theatre productions, and most other forms of entertainment.

In this chapter, students analyze movie advertisements and read both professional movie reviews and those written by students. Students discuss movies they have seen and use a chart to comment on the movie, the plot, the characters and their favorite scene. Students then follow a series of guide questions as they prepare to write a review of a movie they have seen.

Movie reviews are followed by opportunities to write television reviews. With television reviews, the teacher can assign groups of students or the entire class to watch the same shows. Students use the guide questions in the book for class discussion and, ultimately, for writing their own television reviews.

Movie and television reviews are followed by writing restaurant reviews. Again, students have a chance to read restaurant reviews that have appeared in various newspapers. They also have a chance to read restaurant reviews that were written by students. There are discussion questions following each of the reviews.

All these activities culminate in a class project: going to a restaurant for the purpose of reviewing it. The class can be divided into groups and each group may either select a restaurant or be assigned one. Restaurants can include fast-food establishments, as well as more traditional family restaurants. Since the students will go to restaurants as a group, they will have an opportunity to discuss their impressions as they consider guide questions regarding the decor, service, food, price, and so on. This restaurant adventure is followed by having each student write an independent review of the restaurant and rating it.

CHAPTER 9

In this chapter, students begin by learning to write a simple note, messages, and memos. These forms of writing are omitted from most intermediate-level writing textbooks, yet they are important and easy to learn. They also give students a chance to do focused writing.

Create reasons for students to write memos to each other. I suggest bringing in the want ads of newspapers and having students write memos to each other informing them of jobs or merchandise for sale. They may also write memos indicating their reaction to various news, feature, and sports items. You can, of course, use other strategies.

From memo writing, students move on to friendly and formal letter writing. In each case, create real reasons for students to write each type of letter. Create situations that will have an appeal to the students. Suggest that they keep these letters as models that they can refer to in the future. For example, suggest they write to the telephone company explaining that they didn't make the phone calls they were billed for. Have them write to their landlord complaining that they haven't had hot water for three days—and so forth.

CHAPTER 10

In chapter 10, students learn to use comparison and contrast to help them interpret information. They read simple charts taken from the newspaper and they compare and contrast information. More practice can be given to students in this skill by providing them with other similar activities. Material taken from local newspapers or from the school newspaper makes it even more relevant.

The material used in this chapter includes such things as the exchange rate, stock market tables, and airline information.

Sports information such as wins and losses and batting averages can also be used if students have an interest in that area.

CHAPTER 11

In this chapter, students use the material the class has generated all term long to produce a class magazine.

They form an editorial department, an art department, a movie review department, etc. They sort through their writings which gives them a chance to reread their work from the beginning of the term. Seeing how their writing has improved over the course is rewarding and often motivates students to rework their old papers. The added incentive of knowing that some of their papers may be published in the class magazine acts as a further catalyst to self-correct.

This is a good opportunity to focus on editing and proofreading; the students have distance between the time they wrote the essay and the time that they are reading it which gives them greater objectivity; they, also, have a goal of getting their articles published in the class magazine.

Before beginning the project, consider what facilities, if any, are available for the production of the magazine. The magazine can be as elaborate or as simple as you and your facilities allow. If you have a computer system available, determine whether students know how to use it, and whether they will be permitted to use it. You might also check to see whether there is sufficient staffing willing to input the information for the class.

If no computer is available, is there a typewriter and, again, may students use it? And do they know how? If there are no such facilities, do not despair. Some of the loveliest magazines have been done by hand. Is there a student or students who write clearly and beautifully who can hand write the articles? Are there copying facilities or will there be only one glorious magazine or scrapbook with original writings and art work? The key is to motivate and empower the students to use their skills to choose, edit, organize, design, and prepare the final document.

Begin by bringing magazines to class and discussing their content as well as the types of magazines that exist. Most magazines have feature articles, stories, instructions, interviews with famous people, reviews of movies, restaurants and television shows as well as advertisements—all the types of writing students have been doing. Discuss each of the different components of the magazine.

Take advantage of student strengths as much as possible. If you have students with artistic talent spend time talking about the art work in the magazines and how it complements the articles. Discuss advertisements and encourage students to interpret the ads and determine their effectiveness. Ask students to try writing some ads. Encourage them to be creative and write ads for fictional products or parody an ad. These can then be added to the magazine. If time permits and you need money to pay for photo copying etc., you might have students actually ask some of the local businesses in the area to pay for an ad in the student magazine.

Also, have students consider the lay out of some of the magazines. Ask them what the pages look like. Are they balanced and pleasing to the eye? Have students examine the titles and discuss them. You can examine captions and review some of the work you did in earlier chapters. Have students look at the editorial page and read the credits. Discuss what the editor does, the copy editor, the feature editor etc.

If possible, you might also take a field trip to a local magazine or invite a freelance write or editor of a local magazine to visit the class.

Once students have examined magazines and what they consist of, tell them that they will be producing a class magazine using the essays which they have already written. Tell them that like the professional magazines they looked at, their class magazine will also have a variety of articles. To do this they must identify the areas that they will include.

The easiest way to do this is to generate a list on the blackboard of all the subjects students have written about this term. You can use the table of contents or the list provided in chapter 11. Students may want some types of articles and not want others. Leave it up to them.

Next, tell them that they will form committees or departments to work in each of the subject areas they have chosen. Explain that the job of each committee will be to choose the articles to be included in that subject area.

Once all the topics are on the blackboard, suggest that the students include an art department and an editorial department. Explain that the job of the art department will be to enhance the magazine by adding drawings to support the articles, by designing a cover, and by adding artwork wherever appropriate. The art department will work closely with you and the editorial department.

Then explain that the editorial department is in charge of the entire magazine. Explain that this department will work closely under your supervision. They may choose an editor-in-chief or if you wish you may be the editor-in-chief.

In working with the editorial department, be sure that the students choose writing from a variety of students. No student or students should monopolize the articles in the magazine, no matter how good their writing is. Also, every student should play a role in the production of the magazine and get credit for their work.

To choose the title of the magazine you could do brainstorming with the entire class or you can have a contest to see who comes up with the best title. You may offer a prize if you feel it is appropriate. You may also leave the choice of the title up to the editorial department.

Once the title of the magazine has been chosen, the art department can be given the assignment of designing the cover. Then, as the editorial department chooses articles, the articles should be passed along to the art department. The art department will determine what art work, if any, to include.

You may also discuss with the class, as a whole, or leave it up to the editorial department to determine the size of the magazine and how long the entries should be. A story may need more space than a recipe and so on. Students can then be asked to work on condensing the articles they wish to submit to each department. Since condensing is an important writing skill you might want to spend class time on this.

A list of steps to follow for the production of the magazine appear in chapter 11. They can be followed exactly as they appear, or you can supplement them with some of the ideas suggested here.

The extent to which you focus on the development of the magazine depends on the time you have available as well as the resources to type it or to use desk top publishing facilities. The key is to excite the students about seeing their work "published" and to give them opportunities to learn for themselves what goes into producing a class magazine: organization, prioritizing, sharing opinions, working with others, compromising, editing, summarizing, condensing, writing titles, writing captions, adding art, giving credit, proofreading, writing advertisements, comparing articles and selecting the most appropriate, typing, copying, distributing, collating, laughing, worrying, meeting deadlines, etc.

In the end, you will find it well worth the effort. Students have a wonderful sense of accomplishment and they know what it means to work together to produce a final document—their magazine.

To the Student

I wrote this book to make writing in English pleasurable for you. I wanted to motivate you, to challenge you, to give you opportunities to let your personality shine through your writing. I wanted you to look forward to writing, to feel that you were learning a lot, and to feel comfortable writing in English. Most of all, I wanted you to feel confident that you were *ON YOUR WAY TO WRITING* well in English.

There are many creative projects in this book that require you to use your imagination, sense of humor, creativity, and intelligence. To achieve the goals I set forth, I have tried to design writing projects that I think you will enjoy. In *ON YOUR WAY TO WRITING*, you will write fortunes for fortune cookies, restaurant and television reviews, business letters, and notes to friends.

As you work on these projects, you will be asked to keep a journal in which you write to your teacher after each class. In your journal, discuss how you feel about the class, and ask any questions you have about the class or the assignments. The journal is your opportunity to make observations, ask questions, and say what you like or dislike about the class. Your instructor will respond to your questions and comments and clarify information you may not understand. In your journal, you may, of course, write about other subjects which interest you as well.

I think you will enjoy the projects in the book and the opportunity to talk directly to your instructor through the journal. As you work on the assignments, you will gain confidence in your ability as a writer. This will put you *ON YOUR WAY TO WRITING* in English.

ACKNOWLEDGMENTS

Appreciation and recognition go to Kathryn Bonnez for reading the manuscript and offering thoughtful comments, criticisms, and praise.

Rhona B. Genzel

Introduction

Understanding Writing

The goals for this chapter are:

To understand the concept of audience by

- being the audience
- thinking about how we change what we say for different audiences

To understand the differences between writing & speaking

The Concept of Audience

What is writing? How is it different from speaking? These are important questions because most people find it easier to speak than to write. Why do you think that is?

Do you prefer to write or to speak? Why?

In this introduction, we will explore the differences between writing and speaking. This information will help you to think about your reader when you write.

COMMUNICATION EXERCISE 1

Please read the following word out loud:

mym

Notice that different people in the class read it in different ways. Some people may have said "mim," others may have said "mime," and someone may even have said "my m."

However, if you know Russian, you would have said "toot." In the Cyrillic alphabet, "mym" is pronounced "toot" and means "here." What appears to be an "m" in English is a "t" in Russian.

This demonstrates that people who come from different backgrounds can see different things. If people can see different things when they look at a few simple lines in black and white, imagine what happens when they read an entire essay! Keep that in mind as we do the next exercise.

COMMUNICATION EXERCISE 2

Look at the drawing below. What do you see?

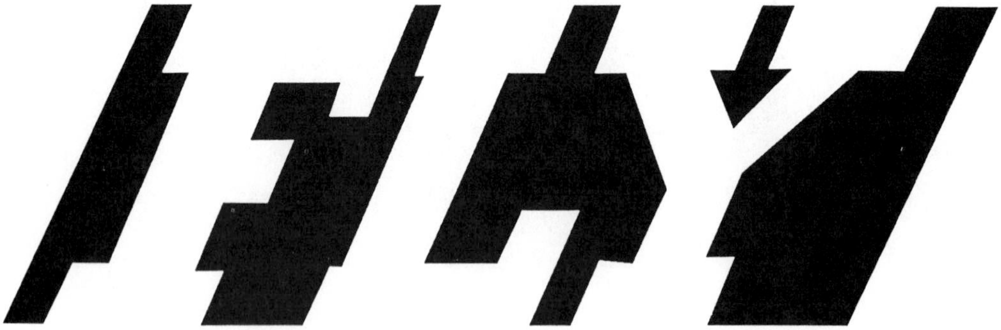

Reprinted, by permission, from *Interactive Techniques for the ESL Classroom*, 47.

Some people will see four black designs on a white background; others will see the word *fly*. What *you* see depends on you. Both of the images are there.

Two people looking at the same thing can see two different things. When we speak, if our listener doesn't understand us, he or she can ask us a question. Our listener's face will tell us that he or she doesn't understand.

We do not have these clues when we write. Therefore, when we write we must be precise. There is no opportunity to ask the reader if he or she understands us or to explain our point in another way.

When we write, we must think about our audience and consider the following:

1. How much does our audience already know about the subject? (If our audience consists of engineers and we are giving a paper on engineering, our language will be highly technical; however, if we are reading a paper on engineering to a group of citizens who are not engineers, the paper will be far less technical.)
2. How old is our audience? (If our audience is made up of children, the language and format will be very different from a presentation to adults.)
3. What is our relationship to the audience? (If we are writing to our boss, our writing will probably be more formal than it would be to a friend.)

COMMUNICATION EXERCISE 3

In addition to thinking about the audience and how much information they already know, we must also be sure that our writing is clear and to the point. If we write about too many things, our reader will become confused.

Look at the drawing below. Try to color in the lines as if you were working in a coloring book.

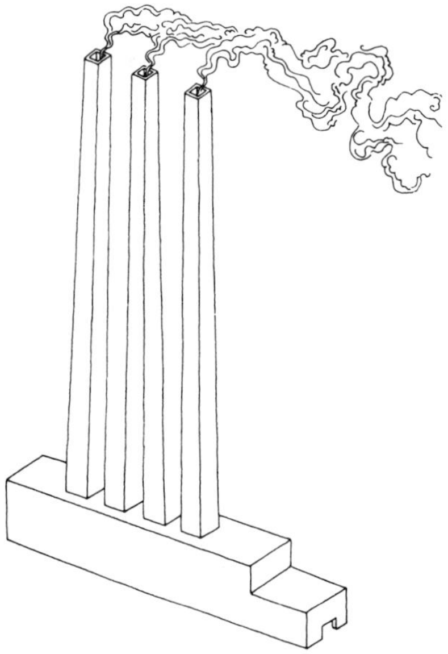

Reprinted, by permission, from *Psychology Today* (February 1984), 80.

What do you notice? Why is it hard to color in the lines? Look at the smokestacks. How many do there appear to be at the top? How many do there appear to be at the bottom? Why does this happen? What has the artist done?

What does this have to do with writing?

It illustrates in black and white what happens when the subject isn't clearly defined or outlined. As writers, artists, or speakers we are communicators. It is our responsibility to be sure that the person we are communicating with understands us. This means that the person understands our idea in the same way that we understand it.

In this book, you will learn how to write clear sentences. You will learn to organize your sentences into meaningful paragraphs, and you will have many opportunities to express yourself—your humor, creativity, ideas, and thoughts—in a variety of written forms.

COMMUNICATION EXERCISE 4

We have said that audience is important and that it influences the way that we write. In the exercise below, we will analyze what is different about various types of writing.

The first column lists various types of writing. Use the second column to write down who the audience would be. In the third column, describe the characteristics that distinguish this type of writing from the other items on the list. Consider the language, the style, the vocabulary, the grammar, and so forth.

Types of writing	*Audience*	*Characteristics*
1. letters home	Mom and Dad	personal, exclamations,
	____________	chatty, informal
2. letters to friends	____________	____________
	____________	____________
3. memos	____________	____________
	____________	____________
4. poems	____________	____________
	____________	____________
5. recipes	____________	____________
	____________	____________
6. directions to your house	____________	____________
	____________	____________
7. telephone messages	____________	____________
	____________	____________

8. resumés	______________	______________
	______________	______________
9. application forms	______________	______________
	______________	______________
10. shopping lists	______________	______________
	______________	______________

Understanding the Differences Between Writing and Speaking

Think about how writing and speaking are different. When we speak, whether it is on the telephone or in person, we can ask questions, make comments, or even make little noises like "hm," "uh huh" to show whether we understand or not. We can laugh, and we can say no. All of these things tell the speaker how well we understand and whether we agree or disagree with what was said. Often, the speaker changes the words or method of presentation to assist the listener. Can you think of any examples of when this happened to you?

If we can see the people we are speaking to, we know whether they understand us by the way they look at us, move their eyes, their mouth, or their body. Think about how people respond when you speak. What facial expressions can you see, and what do these expressions tell you? For example:

- If someone smiles and shakes his head up and down, what does that tell you?
- If the person raises one eyebrow and tilts his head, what does that tell you?
- If the person knits her brow, what does that tell you?
- If the person pouts, what does that tell you?

All of these things happen while you are talking, and they are clues that help you decide how to continue discussing the subject.

How might you change the way you are speaking for each of the responses above?

When we write, we do not have the benefit of knowing how the reader is responding. Knowing the reader's response is very important because as writers we must anticipate what questions the reader may have. We must write clearly so that the reader doesn't have unanswered questions and so that the reader understands our ideas. We must present the information very clearly because there is no chance to say, "Wait a minute, let me explain that better."

Summary of the Differences Between Writing and Speaking

Speaking	*Writing*
1. The audience can ask questions.	The reader cannot ask the author questions.
2. The speaker can watch the listener's face to see if the listener understands.	The writer has no way of knowing if the reader understands.
3. The speaker can correct or make changes as he or she speaks if the speaker thinks the listener doesn't understand.	The writer cannot change what he or she has written.
4. The speaker can use tone of voice, body language, and hand gestures to help the listener understand.	The writer can use only words and punctuation.
5. The speaker can speak quickly or slowly.	The writer doesn't know how fast or slowly the reader is reading.
6. Words disappear "into the air."	Once printed, words can't be erased and rewritten. Writing is a permanent record to be studied, thought about, and enjoyed.

All of these differences mean that the writer must be careful to write clearly in order to be sure there is no opportunity for misunderstanding.

COMMUNICATION EXERCISE 5

In this exercise, we will see how good your communication skills are. You will have an opportunity to give someone instructions and then to follow their instructions. As you do the exercise, think about what might have made it easier for you to follow the directions.

Directions

1. Hide an object somewhere in the building. (You have five minutes to hide it.)
2. Write directions for someone to find the object. (You have fifteen minutes to write the directions.)
3. Exchange directions with someone in your class.
4. Hunt for the object. (You have ten minutes to find it.)

Debriefing

When the ten minutes are up and everyone has returned to the classroom, discuss the experience.

1. Who was the first person to find an object? Why was this person the first one to find the object? Read the directions he or she received. What important information did the writer include?
2. How many other students found an object? What helped them to locate the object?
3. How many students were told in their directions what object they were looking for? Did this help? Why? If you didn't know what you were looking for, would it have helped if the author had told you?
4. Was anyone confused? Why? What would have helped you?
5. What questions do you wish you could have asked the author?
6. Did the author of the directions you followed assume you knew things that you didn't know? Please give examples.
7. What have you learned about writing from this exercise?

Now that you have experienced some of the problems readers have, you will understand why it is important to write very clearly and precisely. Now you recognize the importance of including important details and not assuming that your reader will understand things you have not explained. Below is a list of some of the things you should have learned from the previous exercises.

1. Think about your audience when you write. How much information do they already know? What do they need to know? Who are they?
2. Provide all the information your reader needs. Don't assume that your audience will understand something if you have not explained it.
3. Be specific. Give details.
4. Tell the reader the purpose of your writing at the beginning of your composition.
5. Be clear. Write simply.

Chapter 1

Playing with Sentences

The goals for this chapter are:

To become familiar with three sentence types:

- simple
- compound
- complex

To practice writing all three types of sentences by writing

- captions
- sayings for fortune cookies
- Murphy's laws

As we saw in the Introduction, sometimes when we write, the audience has difficulty understanding our meaning. Sometimes this misunderstanding occurs at the sentence level. If the sentence is unclear or ambiguous, the reader or listener will have trouble understanding what we mean.

Look at the cartoon below and use the guide questions to determine why there was a misunderstanding.

THE WIZARD OF ID — Brant parker and Johnny hart

Reprinted by permission of Johnny Hart and NAS Inc.

Guide Questions

1. Who is the person behind the desk?
2. Who is the other man?
3. What does the other man probably want?
4. Why does the man behind the desk think that the other man writes cookbooks?
5. Why is there a misunderstanding?

What Is a Sentence?

Sentences are the basis of communication in English. A sentence is a group of words with a subject and a predicate that expresses a complete thought or idea.

A subject tells the reader who or what we are talking about. In the first sentence below, the subject is "my brother-in-law."

A predicate tells the reader what the subject does, is doing, will do, has done, or did. In the first sentence below, the predicate is "will attend the banquet."

Sentence Type I—Simple Sentences

In a simple sentence, there is one subject and one predicate.

SENTENCE EXERCISE 1

Read each of the sentences below.

1. My brother-in-law will attend the banquet.
2. The football hero played a very bad game yesterday.
3. His friends were disappointed in his lack of interest in them.
4. Three people died in the accident on the corner of Winton and Elmgrove.
5. The computer is down.
6. John and Jane want to go to the banquet.

Fill in the chart below by indicating the subject, the predicate, and the time of the action.

	Subject	*Predicate*	*Time*
1.	My brother-in-law	will attend the banquet	future
2.	________________	____________________	__________
3.	________________	____________________	__________
4.	________________	____________________	__________
5.	________________	____________________	__________
6.	________________	____________________	__________

SENTENCE EXERCISE 2

Look at the sentences below. For each sentence, ask who or what the sentence is talking about. Draw one line under your answer. That is the subject. Next, ask yourself what the subject is doing, did, or will do. That is the predicate. Draw two lines under the predicate.

1. Americans watch baseball on television.

2. The students studied for their final exams.

3. She called her mother on Monday.

4. The 27″ color television is broken.

5. Both pizza and hamburgers are popular foods in America.

6. The college bookstore has a sale this week.

7. A green Chevrolet hit my car.

8. My favorite rock star will be on television at 11:00 P.M.

SENTENCE EXERCISE 3

In this exercise, you will practice writing simple sentences.

Write a one-word subject next to each number.

For example:

Subject	*Predicate*
1. John	dances well.
2. Paris	is a beautiful city.
3. Eyeglasses	help me see.
4. Democracy	is better than dictatorship.

Write your subjects below. Number 5 should be a person, number 6 should be a place, number 7 an object, and number 8 an idea. Be creative.

5. ______________________________

6. ______________________________

7. ______________________________

8. ______________________________

Exchange your book with another student in the class. Ask your partner to write a predicate next to each subject in order to complete the sentence. Use the examples in the chart above as a model.

SENTENCE EXERCISE 4

In this exercise, you will practice writing more complicated subjects.

This time, next to numbers 6 to 10, write a subject using other words to describe it.

For example:

1. My brother John

2. Paris, the most beautiful city in France,

3. The eyeglasses on the table

4. Democracy in the United States

5. My sisters Jaime and Alison

Exchange books with a classmate. Complete these sentences by writing a predicate for each.

6. ______________________________

7. ______________________________

8. ______________________________

9. ______________________________

10. ______________________________

Reading Captions

In this section, you will have a chance to apply what you have learned and to see how important one or two sentences can be. We will examine captions, which are the sentences written underneath pictures in newspapers and magazines. Captions usually contain one or two sentences that explain the picture.

Look at the pictures below and examine the captions. What does the caption under each picture tell the reader? Is the information important? Would the reader have known this information without the caption?

Fallingwater, designed by Frank Lloyd Wright, has attracted 1,100 visitors daily during its 50th year. Reprinted with permission of the *Times-Union* and *Democrat and Chronicle*, Rochester, NY (October 29, 1989), 6C.

SENTENCE EXERCISE 5

Now let's examine the captions under each picture to see how the newspaper or magazine used the subject and predicate to form good sentences.

For each caption, write the subject and the predicate of the sentence below.

Six one-and-a-half-hour skating sessions are held each Sunday at the Bear Mountain State Park ice rink. Reprinted by permission, from *The New York Times*.

Catfish on ice; 360 million pounds were raised last year. Reprinted, by permission, from *The New York Times*.

Subject (tells who or what the sentence is about)	***Predicate*** (tells what the subject did or is doing)
1. ______	
2. ______	
3. ______	
4. ______	
5. ______	

Remember: Every English sentence has a subject and a predicate.

Kuwaiti volunteers train for combat in the Saudi Arabian desert. Reprinted, by permission, from *Newsweek*.

Janine May, a bodyguard, teaches karate in New Rochelle, N.Y. Reprinted, by permission, from *The New York Times*.

Analyzing Captions

A more careful look at each caption will reveal that sentences have some groups of words that give the reader additional information. This information may tell the reader where or when something took place, or how it happened.

Go back to each caption and see how many of these words you can find. Write these groups of words under the appropriate headings in the chart below.

Caption	*Where*	*When*	*How*
1.			
2.			
3.			
4.			
5.			

SENTENCE EXERCISE 6

Now write a new caption for each of the preceding pictures. Use your imagination. Be sure each sentence has a subject and a predicate.

1. ______
2. ______
3. ______
4. ______
5. ______

SENTENCE EXERCISE 7

Write a caption for each of the pictures below.

Photo by Eddie Hausner, by permission *The New York Times*.

Sentence Type II—Compound Sentences

Sometimes when we write sentences, we want to show that two subjects are doing different things that are related to each other and are of equal importance. This type of sentence has two subjects and two predicates. The sentence expresses one idea, and the two parts of the sentence can stand alone as separate sentences.

For example:

Jim studies psychology, and John studies French.

John and Jim study psychology, but Ann studies engineering.
Jane majored in math, but her brother majored in education.
Susan will visit Mary at the University of Michigan, or Mary will visit Susan at Cornell.

Notice five things:

1. These sentences have two parts.
2. Each part has a different subject and predicate.
3. The two parts are equal in importance.
4. The two parts are joined by a connecting word (and, but, or).
5. Each connecting word has a comma in front of it.

SENTENCE EXERCISE 8

Look at two people in your class. Notice something different about them. Write a sentence about them using the rules above for sentence type II. Continue looking around the room, and write additional sentences on the lines below.

For example:

John is wearing blue jeans, but Alan is wearing a suit.
Mary is looking at Tom, and Tom is looking at Mary.
The window is open, but the door is closed.
I am doing this exercise, but Steve is drawing pictures.
Susan looked at Ellen, and Ellen began to laugh.

1. ______________________________

2. ______________________________

3. ______________________________

4. ______________________________

5. ______________________________

SENTENCE EXERCISE 9

Look at the pictures below, and write a caption for each of them. Most of the pictures have two subjects who are doing different things. Write sentences using two subjects (sentence type II), and the words ***and, but,*** or ***or*** as connecting words.

Wegmans
Clear Plastic Wrap

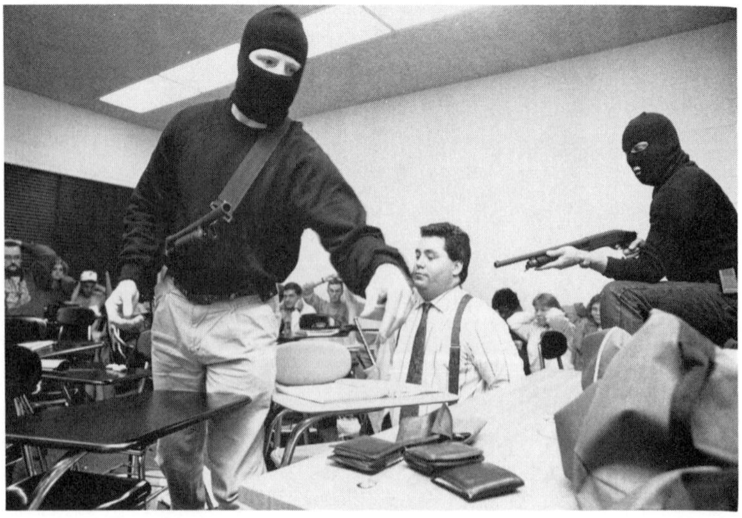

Sentence Type III—Complex Sentences

Sometimes when we write a sentence, it is necessary to show that one idea is dependent on another idea. Look at the following sentence.

If it rains, I will stay home.

This sentence is different from type II. In this sentence, one part of the sentence depends on the other to make sense. Do you know which one depends on the other? How can you tell?

If it rains is not equal to *I will stay home*. *I will stay home* is a complete sentence. If someone says to you *I will stay home*, you will understand them. However, if someone says to you *If it rains*, you will wait to hear what will happen if it rains. The thought is not complete. It does not make sense.

In this type of sentence, one part of the sentence depends on the other in order to be understood.

Here is another example. Pretend that you are talking to a friend, and your friend says:

Whenever my brother plays the drums,

Does this make sense to you? What would you want to know? You would probably want to know what happens when her brother plays the drums.

We could finish the sentence like this:

Whenever my brother plays the drums, my mother closes the door to his room.

What other ways could you finish the sentence? Think of two other possibilities, and write them below.

1. ______________________________

2. ______________________________

SENTENCE EXERCISE 10

Read the following groups of words. Do they make sense? If the sentence is correct, write a "C" next to it. If it isn't correct, what can you add to change it into a sentence that makes sense?

1. When we went to Canada
2. We crossed the Peace Bridge
3. Whenever the telephone rings
4. Since the exam was postponed, we went out to the movies
5. Unless I get the job
6. While you were at school
7. Although my tooth hurts
8. If I get an A in physics
9. Because there is a severe drought in Ethiopia
10. When the team won the game, we cheered
11. Since we were late

Notes

There are four things to remember when you write sentence type III.

1. Sentence type III has two parts, but one part needs the other to express a complete idea.

2. The following words are used in sentence type III to show the relationship between the two parts of the sentence. These words also show that one part of the sentence depends on the other:

when	because
since	while
because	unless
whenever	after
if	before
although	

3. When the above words begin the sentence, use a comma to separate the subject and predicate of the first part of the sentence from the second subject and predicate.
4. When the above words come in the middle of the sentence, do not use a comma.

   For example,

   John comes for dinner whenever my sister is home.
   We will go to the movies unless you have a better suggestion.
   He quit his job because his boss wouldn't give him a raise.

SENTENCE EXERCISE 11

To practice identifying the main and dependent parts of the sentence, draw one line under the subject in each part of the sentence. Draw two lines under the predicate in each part of the sentence. Circle the comma, and put a box around the sentence type III connecting word.

1. Whenever Jim wants to study, his younger brother wants to play with him.
2. Unless I get paid this week, I won't be able to go to the theater with you.
3. If she gets a chance, she should go to New York City.
4. Since the computer was down, I couldn't buy my airline tickets today.
5. Although he had a very good lawyer, the jury found him guilty.
6. Although Susan got three A's, she didn't make the Dean's List.

SENTENCE EXERCISE 12

On the next page is a list of words that are commonly used in type III sentences. Write a sentence for each word. Be sure each sentence has two parts. Be sure that one part of the sentence depends on the other and that the sentence expresses one idea.

when *if* *since* *because* *whenever* *unless* *while*

1. ______________________________

2. ______________________________

3. ______________________________

4. ______________________________

5. ______________________________

6. ______________________________

7. ______________________________

SENTENCE EXERCISE 13

Write a caption for each of the pictures below using the connecting words for type III sentences.

____

Practice with Sentences

As you can see, it is important to be able to write clearly. Have you ever gone to a Chinese restaurant and read your fortune from a fortune cookie? Let's pretend that you have just gotten a job to write the sayings they put into fortune cookies.

Here are some examples to get you started.

You will meet a mysterious stranger.
Your honesty and integrity make all respect you.
Today you will be lucky.

Save your money.
If you are happy, others will be happy too.

Write your fortunes on the lines below. Write some simple, some compound, and some complex sentences. When you are finished, pick two of your favorites and copy them onto a piece of paper. Fold the paper and give it to your teacher, who will put it into a box. Each student will pick a fortune from the box and read it to the class.

1. ______________________________

2. ______________________________

3. ______________________________

4. ______________________________

5. ______________________________

PLAYING WITH SENTENCES

In this exercise, you will write Murphy's laws, building on all the information you learned in this chapter. As you know, there are many laws of science that explain how parts of the universe work. For example:

A body in motion stays in motion.
The shortest distance between two points is a straight line.

There is also Murphy's law. Murphy's law makes fun of things that happen to us in everyday life. They are satirical laws of life based on the idea that

Anything that can go wrong, will go wrong.

These laws of life express frustration about the things that happen to people that they have no control over and that seem unfair.

Many people have come up with their own laws based on the idea that things happen that seem unfair. Read the laws below.

1. "If you are in a hurry, there will be lots of traffic" (Gertrude Beldegreen).
2. "When you have the time to watch television, there are no good shows on" (Brette Genzel).
3. Corollary to number 2: "When you don't have the time to watch television, many good shows are on."
4. "Pills to be taken in twos, always come out of the bottle in threes" (Robert Davis, from Allen L. Otten, *American Way*, September 1978).
5. "The bank's balance is always smaller than yours" (W. W. Chandler, Lyons Kansa, from Allen L. Otten).
6. "Once something is screwed up, anything done to improve it will make it worse" (Jim Russell, *Murphy's Law*, Celestial Arts, Berkeley, CA, 1978, 53).
7. "Fixing a thing takes longer and costs more than you thought" (Russell 53).

8. "If you try to please everybody, nobody will like it" (Russell 55).
9. "If you need a thing, you will have thrown it away" (Russell 55).
10. "If you throw a thing away, you will need it" (Russell 55).
11. "If you keep a thing in case you will need it, you will not need it" (Russell 55).

Now write your own Murphy's laws.

____

____

____

____

____

Chapter 2

Playing with Words and Their Forms

The goals for this chapter are:

To learn word forms

To understand four parts of speech:

- nouns
- verbs
- adjectives
- adverbs

To learn how to identify parts of speech from word endings

Read the sentence below.

The vapy coo desacked the sitar molently. (Anonymous)

Who or what is the sentence talking about? If you said "the vapy coo," you are right. What did the vapy coo do? If you said "desacked the sitar molently," you are right. What word tells you what kind of a coo it is? If you said "vapy," you are right. How did "the vapy coo desack the sitar"? If you said "molently," you are right again.

See how much you already know about the English language!

How did you know all this information? What were the clues? The word *the* tells us that there will be a noun, and the *-ed* at the end of the word *desacked* tells us this word is a verb. The word before a noun usually describes the noun as is the case with *vapy.* Finally, an *-ly* at the end of a word often indicates that the word is what we call an adverb, a word that answers such questions as *how, when,* or *where.*

Do you know what the sentence means? No, of course not. Don't try to understand its meaning. It's nonsense. But it sounds like English, doesn't it? And it sounds like English because it follows the form of English.

In this chapter, we will talk about how to identify words from their endings and how to use words correctly.

WORD DETECTIVE

Below are some sentences that come from student writings. For each sentence, find the word that is incorrectly used. Can you correct it?

1. I am qualified in the area of programming and computer operate.
2. I want to come to your school to become an interior decoration.
3. I believe my educational backgrounds qualify me for the job.
4. I am going to be a hotel management.

When a writer uses the incorrect form of a word, the reader may become confused. To be a good writer, you must learn about the forms of words and when to use them.

In this chapter, you will learn about nouns, verbs, adjectives, and adverbs. You will learn what they are, how to use them correctly, and how to identify them easily.

Being Noun-Wise

Often students who do not understand the different forms words take in English use them incorrectly. In order to use words correctly, it is important to understand their purpose in the sentence.

In the nonsense sentence, the word *coo* told us what the subject was about. It was used as a noun. A noun is a word that names a person, place, thing, or idea.

Read the paragraph below.

In colleges all over the United States, students go to class every day. They try to find knowledge. Sometimes they talk to professors about their courses. At other times they talk about grades.

Now read the paragraph below. Notice that when we change the nouns, the story changes. The time does not change, nor do the descriptions. Notice that we replace nouns with other nouns and that if a noun is singular we replace it with a singular noun. If a noun is plural, we replace it with a plural noun.

After reading the different possible stories, substitute nouns of your own to change the story.

In <u>colleges</u> all over the <u>United States,</u> <u>students</u> go to <u>class</u> every day.

countries	*world*	*people*	*work*
villages	*countryside*	*farmers*	*the fields*
______	________	______	_______

They try to find <u>knowledge.</u> Sometimes they talk to <u>professors</u> about

satisfaction.	*colleagues*
new crops.	*friends*
	workers
________	______

their <u>course.</u> At other times they talk about <u>grades.</u>

work.	*pay.*
boss.	*family.*
crops.	*the weather.*
_____	_________

In the following chart, nouns are grouped by category. Becoming familiar with the different types of nouns will make it easier for you to recognize them.

Person	***Place***	***Thing***	***Idea***
John	Rome	house	democracy
dentist	Florida	computer	love
actor	mall	book	capitalism
biologist	home	chair	opportunity
opportunist	kitchen	pizza	admiration
economist	hall	box	imperialism

NOUN EXERCISE 1

What words from the above chart would you use to fill in the blank spaces in these sentences?

1. My biology professor is a ____________________.

2. Sammy Davis, Jr., was an excellent ____________________.

3. I have a lot of ____________________ for that woman.

4. ____________________ is the capital of Italy.

Noun Endings

Now go back to the chart, and look at the words in the columns marked *person, place, thing,* and *idea.* Notice that in some of the columns the words end in the same way. In this section, we will examine the endings of nouns and what they mean. The endings of words can tell you a lot about the word. Below are some common noun endings and their meanings.

-er, -eer, -or: These endings mean someone who or something that does something.

For example, a toaster is something that toasts bread; a waiter is someone who waits on tables. Look at the list of words below ending in *-er, -eer,* and *-or.* What do you know about each word? Guess each word's meaning, and write the meaning in the space provided.

Noun	*Meaning*
professor	someone who teaches
writer	someone who writes
engineer	someone who constructs things
calculator	something that calculates things
counselor	____________________
photographer	____________________
painter	____________________
printer	____________________
editor	____________________
lawyer	____________________

decorator	______________
philosopher	______________
employer	______________
settler	______________
collector	______________
computer	______________
amplifier	______________

-ess is an ending that also means someone who does something, but it refers to a female. Below are words ending with *-ess*. Write the meaning in the space provided.

Noun	***Meaning***
waitress	______________
actress	______________
stewardess	______________
duchess	______________
heiress	______________
princess	______________

-ist also refers to a person. When you see *-ist* at the end of a word you should know that the word means someone who does something. Write the meaning in the space provided.

Noun	***Meaning***
biologist	someone who studies biology
artist	______________
segregationist	______________
opportunist	______________
optimist	______________

pessimist	______________________
feminist	______________________
cartoonist	______________________
chemist	______________________
pharmacist	______________________
specialist	______________________
orthodontist	______________________

Even though many of these words are advanced-level words, you will recognize them as nouns, and you will know that they mean someone who or something that does something. You will know that each time you see *-er, -eer, -or, -ess,* or *-ist,* the word is a noun and therefore the name of a person, place, thing, or idea.

NOUN EXERCISE 2

Use what you have learned about word endings to complete this exercise. Hint: each sentence needs a noun ending with *-ist.*

1. A ______________________ is someone who studies biology.
2. A ______________________ is someone who studies chemistry.
3. An ______________________ is someone who studies art.
4. A ______________________ is someone who draws cartoons.
5. An ______________________ is the opposite of a pessimist.

NOUN EXERCISE 3

Use the following nouns in a sentence of your own.

calculator	toaster	storekeeper
engineer	employer	heater
doctor	carburetor	air conditioner
computer	tape recorder	actor

1. ______________________
2. ______________________
3. ______________________

4. ______________________________

5. ______________________________

6. ______________________________

7. ______________________________

8. ______________________________

9. ______________________________

10. ______________________________

11. ______________________________

12. ______________________________

Other nouns that refer to ideas end in *-ism, -ness, -tion, -ment, -ency, -ancy, -ance,* and *-ence.* Examples of words with these endings are below. These endings do not indicate a person or thing but rather an idea or concept.

NOUN EXERCISE 4

-ism means the act, practice, or result of doing something.

Noun	*Meaning*
mannerism	______________
opportunism	______________
communism	______________
racism	______________
favoritism	______________
idealism	______________
cannibalism	______________

Look up the meaning of these words in a dictionary. Write the meaning of each word in the space provided.

Notice how these words might be used in sentences.

1. The teacher showed favoritism toward Susan.
2. She had the strange mannerism of tapping her finger on the desk when she was nervous.

NOUN EXERCISE 5

-ness names the way something is, or its condition.

Noun	*Meaning*
shyness	____________________
dryness	____________________
happiness	____________________
sadness	____________________
calmness	____________________
fondness	____________________
softness	____________________

Try to guess the meaning of these words. Write their definitions in the space provided. Do the same thing for Noun Exercises 6, 7, and 8, which follow.

NOUN EXERCISE 6

-tion indicates an action or the act of doing something.

Noun	*Meaning*
illumination	the act of adding light
comprehension	____________________
admiration	____________________
formation	____________________
dedication	____________________
conception	____________________
cancellation	____________________
celebration	____________________
invitation	____________________
graduation	____________________

NOUN EXERCISE 7

-ment indicates a result or a product.

Noun	*Meaning*
management	______________________
settlement	______________________
predicament	______________________
entertainment	______________________
amendment	______________________
discouragement	______________________
endowment	______________________

NOUN EXERCISE 8

-ency, -ancy, -ance, -ence means the act of, quality, result, or degree

Noun	*Meaning*
circumstance	______________________
urgency	______________________
abundance	______________________
deliverance	______________________
remembrance	______________________
attendance	______________________
grievance	______________________
compliance	______________________
presidency	______________________
consistency	______________________
hesitance	______________________
difference	______________________

NOUN EXERCISE 9

Fill in the blanks with words from the lists in exercises 1 through 8.

1. There is no place in the world for people who believe in ______________________.
2. The USSR followed the theory of ______________________.
3. He smiles in a strange way. It is an odd ______________________.
4. He got a cold from the ______________________ in the cellar.
5. Did you get an ______________________?
6. His ______________________ has been poor. He came to only half the classes.
7. Our garden produced an ______________________ of apples. It's more than we can eat. Please take some.

NOUN EXERCISE 10

Categorize the following nouns by putting them in the appropriate columns below.

cartoonist	amendment	presidency	duchess
philosopher	scientist	lawyer	writer
propeller	singer	broiler	printer
corner	democracy	argument	London

Person	*Place*	*Thing*	*Idea*
________	________	________	________
________	________	________	________
________	________	________	________
________	________	________	________

NOUN EXERCISE 11

Read the sentences below, and determine what the difference in meaning and purpose is for each of the underlined words.

1. The <u>management</u> was angry.
2. The <u>manager</u> was angry.

3. The collector exhibited his antiques.
4. The collection of Monet's artwork is at the gallery.

5. The amplifier gives sufficient amplification.

6. The editor made many changes in the manuscript.
7. The book went into its third edition.

8. The entertainment in Las Vegas is outstanding.
9. The entertainer received a high salary.

NOUN EXERCISE 12

Now that you understand that nouns serve different purposes and that noun endings tell the reader important information, try the game below.

This is a competitive game. You will have three minutes to write as many nouns as you can think of that end in *-ist* and *-er*.

-ist *words*	-er *words*
1. ______	
2. ______	
3. ______	
4. ______	
5. ______	
6. ______	
7. ______	
8. ______	

NOUN EXERCISE 13

Each of the sentences below has an incorrect form of a word. Find the words and write the correct form.

1. I am going to be a hotel management. ______
2. Jan is a good employment. ______
3. His happy makes me happy. ______
4. He is a collection of antiques. ______
5. His shy was a problem. ______

NOUN EXERCISE 14

Read the sentences below. In each sentence, one of the nouns is in an incorrect form. See if you can find the incorrect form and change it to singular or plural. Information about singular and plural nouns follows this exercise. After reading the information, you can return to this exercise and complete it.

1. Wendy moved in and threw my stuffs in the hallway.
2. I saw a couple of my friend.
3. It was another one of those typical college weekend.
4. We will visit several different printing plant.
5. Cities have noisy, rushing crowd of people.
6. The porter unloaded our baggages.
7. It is one of the biggest company in my country.

WORD DOCTOR

When we talk about more than one thing, we usually add an *-s* or *-es* to the end of the noun. Students often have difficulty remembering to use a plural in sentences like these:

1. It was one of the hardest tests I have ever taken.

This sentence talks about one of many tests. The writer may be talking about one test, but he or she is comparing it to a lot of other tests that he or she has taken.

2. Hunger is one of the major problems in the world today.

The same idea applies here. Hunger is one of many major problems.

When you use the following expressions, follow them with the plural form of the noun as in the sentences above.

one of
many of the
some of the
a lot of the
none of the

Some words do not change whether they are singular or plural. They keep the same form. The best way to learn them is to memorize them. The list below shows some of these words. After you have reviewed it, go back and correct the sentences in noun exercise 14.

homework	rice
equipment	information
baggage	luggage
machinery	advice
stuff	money
fruit	food
furniture	ignorance

Being Verb-Wise

Read the sentence below.

The child eppified on his way to school.

The word *eppified* isn't a word in English. What purpose does it serve in the sentence? If you answered that it tells the reader what the subject did, you are right. It tells the reader two things. It tells what the child did, and it tells us that the time is past. It is the verb in the sentence.

Verbs are words that identify the action in the sentence and that tell us when the action occurred. Some verbs such as *be* (*is, are, was, were*) give us state of being.

Below are some sentences from student writing. Each has an error. Can you identify the mistake and correct it?

1. I arrangement the entire party.

2. The alumnus endorsement a large check to the university.

Verbs tell us the time when the action in the sentence happened. Here are examples of verbs as they are used in English sentences. Can you tell when the action took place? Write the time in the column to the right of the sentence. The first one has been done for you.

In English you can easily identify the verbs in a sentence by:

1. the endings (*-ed, -ing*)
2. the words that come before the verb (may be the following: *has, have, had, is, are, was, were, will, have had, has had, had had, had been,* etc.)
3. the fact that verbs usually indicate the action in the sentence

Sentences	*Time*
1. I am studying English in the United States.	present or current
2. I work at a department store.	________________
3. I went to London last year.	________________
4. I have been studying English for two months.	________________
5. I will study French next year.	________________

Verb Endings

Usually when we think of verb endings, we think about adding *-ed* to make the past tense of a verb, or we think about irregular forms such as "have eaten," "had been." We also may think about adding an *-s* for the third person singular "he walks," "she goes." But there are also word endings that tell us that a particular word is a verb. In fact, these endings can be used to change words into verbs.

In English, words that are not verbs can often be changed into verbs by adding a special verb ending. There are four verb endings:

-fy
-ify
-ize
-ate

VERB ENDING EXERCISE 1

When you see the above endings on a word, you can assume that the word is a verb. Note the examples of some of these verbs below. Fill in the chart by providing the meaning and the appropriate form of the verbs listed. Look up each word in a dictionary and write its meaning in the space provided. The first one has been done for you.

Verb	*Meaning*	*Past*	*Future*	*Present Perfect*	*Present Continuous*
meditate	think deeply about something	meditated	will meditate	has meditated	is meditating
organize ______					
evaporate ______					
specialize ______					
testify ______					
verify ______					
motivate ______					
anticipate ______					
equalize ______					
negate ______					

VERB ENDING EXERCISE 2

In this exercise, you will practice using verbs that have been formed from other words.

Word	*Verb Form*
real	realize
beauty	beautify
actual	actualize

Write a sentence for each verb. Use different times in your sentences (present, past, future, etc.).

1. ______________________________

2. ______________________________

3. ______________________________

NOUN/VERB EXERCISE 1

One word may have a variety of forms depending on its use in the sentence. The verb may be *walked,* but the noun might be *walker,* meaning something that helps someone walk or someone who walks.

Noun	*Verb*
amendment	amend
cancellation	cancel
administration	administer
attendance	attend
comprehension	comprehend

Write sentences for each of the verbs and nouns listed above.

1. ______________________________

2. ______________________________

3. ______________________________

4. ______________________________

5. ______________________________

6. ______________________________

7. ______________________________

8. ______________________________

9. ______________________________

10. ______________________________

WORD FORM GAME

This game can be played with the entire class as one big group, or the class can be divided into small groups.

Choose one student to leave the room for a few minutes. While the student is outside, the class or group must choose a word which is either a noun or a verb. Once the class has agreed on one word, the student may return to class. It is the job of the student to guess the word the class chose by asking the class questions that require a yes or no answer. She/he may ask questions such as:

Is it a verb?
Is it a noun?
Does it name a person?
Is it a word expressing past time?
Is it in this room?
Do you do it?

NOUN AND VERB IDENTIFICATION EXERCISE

Read the article below, and write the nouns and verbs in the margin on each side.

Nouns	Article	*Verbs*
	Agile robot treads where humans fear **By Phil Ebersole** Democrat and Chronicle An agile robot designed by Jean Du Teau of Rochester Robotics Inc. goes into the radioactive steam generators of nuclear power plants to inspect and retrieve debris. It is used by R. Brooks Associates, a nuclear engineering service firm in Rochester, as part of its service. The robot, controlled from 100 feet away, can enter a six-inch diameter hole, go deeply into the nuclear vessel and make up to three 90-degree turns, said John Gay, one of the five partners in R. Brooks. The robot, which unfolds to a 15-inch diameter once it's inside, can carry a TV camera for inspection and a grabber to retrieve a piece of debris that's fallen into the vessel, he said. Ralph Hansen, director of general engineering for Duquesne Light Co. of Pittsburgh, one of R. Brooks' customers, said inspection would be much more difficult without this technology. Reactors used by Duquesne were designed at a time when nuclear engineers didn't realize they'd be inspected as often as they are, he said. So inspection, while possible, is difficult and inconvenient. The new	

robot "gives a much better view and perspective of what's going on," he said.

One of the big advantages of R. Brooks' robot is that it minimizes exposure to nuclear radiation of plant workers. "Because of radiation, it's important you use equipment rather than personnel."

Du Teau has two businesses at 1225 Jefferson Road in Henrietta—Robot World, a retail store, and Rochester Robotics, a wholesale, service and design company. It's one of a few firms that specializes in service robots as distinguished from those used in manufacturing.

Being Adjective-Wise

An adjective is a word that describes a noun. For example:

I took a difficult test.

The adjective is *difficult.* It describes the test. Now look at this sentence.

I took a long and difficult test.

In this sentence, the word *difficult* describes the noun *test.* It was a difficult test. The word *long* also can describe the word *test.*

It was a long test.

Both the word *long* and the word *difficult* are adjectives.

Adjectives add important information to your writing. For example:

The yellow and green butterfly flew away.
Do you know where my brown socks are?
I'm looking for the big black suitcase.

ADJECTIVE EXERCISE 1

In each of the above sentences, the adjective is necessary in order for the listener or speaker to know which object the person means. Can you name the adjectives in each of the sentences above?

ADJECTIVE EXERCISE 2

Adjectives add important information and spirit to our writing. Notice the difference between

The boy sat down.

and

The tall, thin, nervous boy sat down.

Notice how much more interesting and meaningful the sentence has become. Now read this sentence.

The student took the test.

and

The silly but hopeful student took the Spanish test.

or

The serious and nervous student took the easy calculus test.

What have we learned that we didn't know before?

Notice how the sentence below can be improved by adding a few adjectives.

He took the ______________________ test.

hard
easy
impossible
tricky
history
long

What do each of these words tell the reader? How do they improve the sentence?

Find sentences with adjectives in books and magazines. Copy them here. Circle each adjective. Be prepared to explain why it is important.

____

____

____

____

____

____

____

____

____

____

____

ADJECTIVE EXERCISE 3

Often students say that they don't know how to add more specific details to their writing. One good way to do this is to add adjectives. Adjectives give the reader colorful information to help the reader see what the writer is discussing.

Read the sentences below.

1. A boy rushed into the cafeteria and put some food on his tray. He paid the cashier and sat down to eat.

Now, read sentence 2 below.

Then replace some of the underlined words in number 2 with words of your choice to create a completely different paragraph. Notice how changing the adjectives alters the paragraph. Also notice how the story changes.

2. The tired and hungry boy rushed into the crowded cafeteria.

____ ____ ____

He paid the young and beautiful cashier and sat down to eat.

____ ____

How have the sentences been changed? Which set of sentences gives the reader more information?

Now read the rest of the description.

He grabbed a green tray and took a tuna fish sandwich, a glass of chocolate milk, a yellow banana, and a huge chocolate ice cream cone, and ran to the busy cashier. He gave her three dollars, took plastic silverware, and began to look for a seat. He found an empty seat at a table with three noisy guys and two bored girls. He put his big green book bag on the cluttered floor and sat down in the empty seat. As he began to eat his food, one of the girls said, "I'm sorry, but this seat is taken."

Notice how the adjectives add information that helps the reader "see" the room and the people.

Comprehension Questions

1. What do we know about the boy?
2. Do you think the seat was really taken? Maybe they didn't want him to sit there. What do you think?

ADJECTIVE EXERCISE 4

The sentences below come from student essays. Each has an error. Can you identify the mistake?

1. I have taken courses in varies languages.
2. It didn't take long before I was in a depth sleep.
3. The contentment people gave the waiter a big tip.

Endings for Adjectives

Ending	*Meaning*	*Examples*
-able, -ible	capable of	breakable, possible, inflatable
-al	of, belonging to, part of	natural
-est	most, highest	best, softest, biggest, hardest, smartest
-ful	full of	careful, youthful, skillful
-ial	of, pertaining to	facial, spacial
-ic, -ical	of, like	comic, comical
-ile	of, pertaining to	infantile, percentile
-ine	to be like	feminine
-ish	characteristic of	selfish, childish, Turkish, Spanish
-lent	full of	excellent
-less	without	painless, toothless
-ous	full of	generous, marvelous
-y	pertaining to	creamy, icy, spicy

When you see these endings on words, you will know that most of the time they are adjectives. Knowing this will help you to use them correctly.

ADJECTIVE EXERCISE 5

Circle the adjectives.

1. He received the highest score.
2. It was a painless operation.
3. The creamy chocolate cake is my favorite.
4. The car looks fabulous with those new blue seat covers.
5. He was not careful with the breakable bottle.
6. The spicy chicken was delicious.
7. The large man with the scrawny beard gave us a big, toothless grin.
8. The sugarless drink was tasteless.

WORD-WISE

In the sentences below, students have invented or misused words. Can you identify and correct them?

1. I am happy to see a job listed in the displacement office.

2. The take his or her pictures ugly.

3. I am worried about my schedule because I don't want a confrontation with my business class.

4. The author describes how the grandmother is possessive, strong, and humoristic.

5. I can adjust myself to the cultural here.

ADJECTIVE EXERCISE 6

Look around the room. Look at each other. Look out the window and list some of the things you see. Since all these words NAME something they will be nouns.

For example, you might write *chair, classmate, book, window, light,* etc. These are some of the things that you see. What can you say about each of these things?

Perhaps the chair is *old, new, brown,* or *shiny.* All of these words describe it. Maybe it is *dirty* or *clean.* For each of the words you wrote, list several words that describe it.

1. ____________	4. ____________
____________	____________
____________	____________
____________	____________
2. ____________	5. ____________
____________	____________
____________	____________
____________	____________
3. ____________	6. ____________
____________	____________
____________	____________
____________	____________

ADJECTIVE EXERCISE 7

Now divide into groups and have each group choose something to describe. Your teacher may choose to assign each group a category.

For example, things found in an office.

If you choose the word *telephone,* here are some words you could use to describe it.

Telephone

black
plastic
old
new
loud
square
large

Now that you understand what to do, decide on something to describe and see how many adjectives you can list to describe it. Think of as many words as you can and write them below for your word.

Name of object ____________

1. ____________

2. ____________

3. ______________________________

4. ______________________________

5. ______________________________

6. ______________________________

7. ______________________________

8. ______________________________

9. ______________________________

10. ______________________________

Now choose an actor or actress to describe. ______________

1. ______________________________

2. ______________________________

3. ______________________________

4. ______________________________

5. ______________________________

6. ______________________________

7. ______________________________

8. ______________________________

9. ______________________________

10. ______________________________

ADJECTIVE EXERCISE 8

How many adjectives can you think of to describe the words listed below? You can divide into groups and see which group can write down the most adjectives in ten minutes, or you can do the exercise on your own.

Test *Neighbor*

1. ______________________________

2. ______________________________

3. ______________________________

4. ______________________________

5. ______________________________

6. ______________________________

7. ______________________________

8. ______________________________

9. ______________________________

10. ______________________________

11. ______________________________

12. ______________________________

13. ______________________________

14. ______________________________

15. ______________________________

16. ______________________________

17. ______________________________

18. ______________________________

19. ______________________________

20. ______________________________

Being Adverb-Wise

An adverb usually answers these questions: Where? When? Why? How? How much? or How long? Adverbs tell us more about verbs, adjectives, or other adverbs.

For example:

Where?

He went *outside*.
He sat *there*.

When?

He came *immediately*.
She will pay *later*.
The magazine comes *monthly*.

How?

He ran *quickly*.
They danced *beautifully*.
They worked *tirelessly*.

How much or how long?

She *almost* caught the ball.
The hotel was *near*.

When you look at these adverbs, do you see one ending that appears often? If you said "-ly," you are right. The ending *-ly* often indicates that a word is an adverb.

ADVERB EXERCISE

Here is a list of adjectives. Add *-ly* to each word to make it into an adverb.

Adjective	*Adverb*
serious	______________
timid	______________
quiet	______________
cautious	______________
exceptional	______________
usual	______________
unusual	______________
careful	______________
brave	______________
quick	______________
dangerous	______________

WORD FORM APPLICATION EXERCISE

Now that you understand nouns, verbs, adjectives, and adverbs, read the paragraph below. Then, expand upon these sentences by adding or changing words to create a more interesting story. Write the words you are changing or modifying on the space below each line. Consider what information you can add to this story to make it more interesting. Add adjectives and adverbs, and change the nouns and verbs to make them more specific.

I was driving down a street. When I stopped for a red light, the car be-

____

hind me hit my car. My bumper and fender were damaged in the acci-

____

dent. The passenger in the other person's car had to go to the hospital.

____

We called the police from a house nearby, and when the policewoman

____

came, she gave the driver of the other car a ticket. He was a big man, and

____

he got so angry that he started kicking the tires on his car. I was glad the

____

police were there because this man frightened me.

____

Chapter 3

Capturing the Main Idea

The goals for this chapter are:

To learn to focus

To write concisely

To capture the main idea

To write summaries

To combine sentences

Writing in English is different from writing in other languages. Writers of English try to use few words to express an idea, and they are specific in saying exactly what they mean. Sometimes their directness appears strange or even rude to people who are accustomed to using a less direct method in their own language.

Since being direct and succinct is not customary in many parts of the world, we will practice it in this chapter. One way to practice capturing the main idea and saying it in as few words as possible is to write newspaper headlines. Newspaper headlines must tell the reader what the article is about in seven words or less. The reader can then choose to read the article for more detailed information.

In this chapter, you will have an opportunity to read some newspaper headlines and to understand why they were selected. You will see how the headlines tell the reader what the article will be about in very few words. Once you understand how the headlines are written, you will have an opportunity to write headlines of your own. Then you will practice expanding this concept to writing summaries and learn how to use sentence combining as a technique to condense information.

A newspaper has limited space, and it must find a way to attract the reader's attention and provide sufficient information to make the reader want to read the story. The article below explains how newspaper headlines are written. Read it, and be prepared to answer the comprehension questions that follow the article.

Telling stories in seven words or less
Letter to the reader

Ray Gniewek

Ray Gniewek is copy chief for the *Democrat and Chronicle.*

Headlines are basically advertisements for stories. Some sell the steak (facts) and some sell the sizzle (mood).

They are a form of writing found nowhere outside the confines of newspaper columns. They use present tense to describe the past, and throw out adjectives, conjunctions and other niceties for the sake of space. Headlines don't stop when they have nothing left to say, they stop when their allotted space is filled.

It is not enough that a headline makes sense, it also must look good. Each of its lines must be of roughly equal length. And, just as poems have rhyme schemes, a headline is structured: Lines must not split verbs, nor should they split adjectives from nouns. Ideally, one line equals one thought.

The goal for a copy editor, the person who writes the headline, is to reflect a story: its content, its tone, preferably both.

A straight headline summarizes. An earthquake shakes Turkey and kills 10 people. The headline:

Quake kills 10 in Turkey

If there is not enough space for that, then specifics must be dropped:

Quake kills 10

These straight heads reflect content.

But a headline can go beyond the obvious and catch both the facts of a story and its tone. Just such a head was written by veteran copy editor Herm Archunde. He was faced with a story about President Carter and Sen. Ted Kennedy meeting at the White House and basically agreeing to nothing. Herm came up with:

Carter, Ted meet,
but minds don't

How about a head that catches a tone. Monday we had a story about a man who lost his wife to cancer and the next day his son was shot and killed. A straight head might have been:

Man mourns deaths of wife, son

But Maurice Handy, a young copy editor from Missouri, chose to capture the story's emotions. He wrote:

'Wherever I go, whatever I do, I'll cry'

It doesn't have a who, what, when, where or why, but it makes you wince. And suffering was the essence of the story.

Some stories are just plain funny. Headlines for these call for a clever approach: a pun, a riddle, a play on words or a play on a cliche.

When the zebra at the Seneca Park Zoo gave birth on the 4th of July, Jody McPhillips wrote a flag-waver to describe the newborn:

A star
in stripes
forever

(McPhillips, a newcomer to Rochester, earned her editing stripes in Elmira.)

But there are limits to our humor. We don't play with a person's name or try to be funny in a story where somebody died or was hurt.

As you can see, writing a headline can be frustrating. Copy editors are often tempted to simply write:

Good story below

But we resist the temptation. We're obligated to tell you more than that.

At times we want to tell you to read a story very carefully. When Cyrus Vance quit as secretary of state, the initial stories were based on reports from State Department insiders. There was no guarantee the reports were accurate (events proved they were). What kind of headline tips off the reader that a story may not be the gospel?

There are many techniques. The first is the question mark:

Vance to quit?

The second is the "may" head:

Vance may quit

A third technique is to use attribution, but as you can see the head grows longer:

Vance to quit, sources say

A fourth technique is to use "reportedly":

Vance reportedly to quit

Don't just go by what the head says to determine a story's importance. Is the head big or small, at the top of the page or bottom? This tells you something of the opinion of the news editor, who will read, judge and weigh more stories in a day than most people will in a month.

Headline punctuation differs greatly from that used in common writing. If you've been reading papers for a few years, you probably recognize some quirks. For example, we use single quotation marks (') instead of two ("), and we don't use periods to end headlines. Here's a brushup lesson on a few other oddities:

- The colon: The most common use of a colon is when it stands for "said."

Carter: Get out of Afghanistan

It is also used when the word before the colon is a topic:

Inflation: Carter's big problem

- The long dash. This also stands for "said":

Get out of Afghanistan—Carter

This is a more alien style. It is usually unattractive and we try to avoid it. However, it has saved more than one editor from a white-out.

- The comma. In headlines, the comma replaces "and." Instead of writing, "A child and seven others are hurt in a fire," we write:

Child, 7 hurt in fire

This is dangerous because, to the casual reader, it looks very much like:

Child, 7, hurt in fire

And if the copy editor is sleepy and his boss is dopey we may leave the reader grumpy with the ambiguous construction:

Fire hurts child, 7

- Quotation marks not only indicate what someone said, they are used in this type of construction:

'Sex scandal' investigated

The quotation marks mean someone believes there is a sex scandal. The quotation marks are saying: Don't necessarily take this literally.

Comprehension Questions

1. What is a copy editor?

____

2. When do headlines stop?

____

3. Where are headlines found?

____

4. In addition to making sense, headlines must also ______________.

5. Can headlines reflect humor?

____

6. Can headlines convey feelings?

____

7. What methods do newspapers use to indicate that a headline may not be true?

____

Recognizing That Headlines Aren't Always Sentences

In chapter 1, we learned that a sentence has a subject and a predicate and expresses one idea. Headlines are not always written as sentences. Because of space problems, the newspaper may omit some words. Look at each of the headlines below, and determine if it is a sentence or not. If it is a sentence, write the word *sentence* under it. If it isn't a sentence, fix it.

1. Telling stories in seven words or less

____

2. Quake kills 10 in Turkey

____

3. Quake kills 10

____

4. Carter and Ted meet, but minds don't

---

5. Man mourns death of wife and son

---

6. Wherever I go, and whatever I do, I'll cry

---

7. A star in stripes forever

---

8. Good story below

---

9. Vance may quit

---

10. Carter: Get out of Afghanistan

Writing Headlines

Now that you understand how headlines are written, you will have an opportunity to write a headline. The newspaper that ran the article about writing headlines also ran a contest to see who could write the best headline for a story. Read the contest rules below. Then write a headline for the story.

The newspaper awarded a $25 prize for the best headline, but that contest was a long time ago. Maybe your teacher will offer a reward or prize to someone in the class who creates the best headline.

Write one and win $25

So you'll appreciate how hard it can be to write a headline, we're sponsoring a contest. We'll supply the story, you supply the headline. You must write two lines, each counting between 15–17 units.

Reprinted with permission of the *Times-Union* and *Democrat and Chronicle*, Rochester, NY (August 1980).

To count: Lower case letters count one, as do spaces between words. However, lower case m and w count 1½, as do all caps, except M and W, which count 2. Commas, colons, semi-colons and quotation marks count ½, while question marks and long dashes count 1½.

The story:

GENEVA, Switzerland—Swiss tradesmen are going for the world's record for the longest sandwich, but they're making it of ham . . . and holding the Swiss.

The contestants said the sandwich, which they plan to put together Saturday, will be 590 feet long, which is 10 feet longer than the longest sandwich recognized by the Guinness Book of World Records. *The Geneva sandwich will comprise 1,400 pounds of bread, 460 pounds of ham and 240 pounds of butter. It will be built along a pedestrian street in downtown Geneva.*

When the contest was over, the newspaper printed the headlines that the public had submitted. These headlines are provided below. Read them and determine which ones you like and why. Then share your headline with the class.

Hold the mail, we've got a winner

By Ray Gniewek

D&C Copy Chief

Readers—and I'm stealing one of your lines—I've got to ham it to you. Your headlines kept me laughing for two days.

There were 675 pieces of mail for the headline contest and those contained more than 800 entries. Most of the entries were good, many very good, quite a few great.

The idea that caught the fancy of many of you was: Swiss ham it up.

It's a solid idea. The it can refer to the sandwich or the whole line can refer to the attitude of the Swiss tradesmen in promoting such an event.

Now, from that start, here are some of the better variations:

Paul Zwick of Rochester needed a pun:

Kneading record
Swiss ham it up

Jim Early of Clyde, who said, "I imagine you will receive several of the same," was wrong about the bottom line:

Swiss ham it up
to great lengths

Mrs. Eleanore Bauer of Fairport and Rochester's Barbara Ciavarri and Elizabeth Krueger of Giffard all came up with the following independently:

Swiss ham it up;
all holes barred

All told, there must have been nearly 100 headlines on the Swiss ham it up theme. Including one from William Lombard, former sheriff of Monroe County. Although he captured the gist of the story he didn't nab the prize with:

Swiss, ham it up
For world record

And Buz Orlopp of Williamson didn't err at all with:

For the record,
Swiss ham it up

Every one of the above would have gotten in the paper. Each is good.

But now, the winner:

Swiss cram ham;
no holes in plan

It was submitted by Herbert W. Horton of Webster who wins the $25 prize.

Why this one over the hundreds of others? Because I like the "am" sound of cram ham, and the bottom line has two meanings: One, that the line was well thought out, which it was. Secondly, it plays with the idea that there was no Swiss cheese in sight.

It has drawbacks, too. No hint that a record is up for grabs, let alone the idea of a giant sandwich.

But then every headline is a compromise. And that is probably the most important lesson our contest taught.

Kathy Bills of Webster learned it well. She wrote:

What at first seemed to be a relatively easy task did indeed turn out to be quite challenging.

Every "brilliant" thought inevitably was over/under the count. Then, when trying to alter the words—the text was lost.

The difficulties were not lost on Jeanne A. Weintraub of Penfield either:

Most of my wildly creative ideas ended up in the "round file." They were ruled out because they couldn't meet the rigid specifications.

Suddenly, the full impact of the difficulties of your work hit me . . .

In Hammondsport, Arlene Bradstreet and Anne Bradstreet Grinols were beaten by the difficulties:

After pages and pages of trys, I mean tries, we came to the conclusion that we could take on the job of headline writer providing all paper was supplied, we could take forever, and we could be paid by the hour.

Headline writers do get all the paper they need and do get paid by the hour, but they can't take forever. If they take longer than about 15 minutes that's too long.

Their heads come to me on a computer terminal, which is programmed to count each headline, taking the drudgery out of counting.

Your entries came in every form. They were handwritten, personally typed, typed by your secretary (naughty). They were on post cards, plain white paper, floral stationery and office stationery (naughty).

But one person robbed a scene from an old gangster film and sent his entry with individually cut out letters from the paper. A masterful job and not a bad head:

Swiss sandwich
sorta ham on wry

But the perpetrator of this headline, which I almost mistook as a ransom note, went awry and made one error. A gummed address sticker. We know who you are, Karl E. Bailey, and on what street in Rochester you live.

While Karl was cutting and pasting, whole families were entering. Mrs. Genevieve Tassone wrote that "my daughter, granddaughter & grandma are competing!"

Others included an entry from each member of the family as did the Hartzells of Penfield.

Some people sent in dozens of entries (26 by Sharon Bloemendaal of Rochester). Some sent in a new entry each time they had a better headline, such as Sandi Helfand, another Rochesterian.

Never give up, that's admirable. Copy editors at the *D&C* often change headlines when they get a better one.

I never realized there were so many names for a, well, er, what am I to call it? Sandwich, grinder, hero, hoagie, torpedo or sub? I guess it all depends on where you are from.

But for the purposes of a headline what would you choose?

Sub and hero seem to work best for the purposes of word play.

My favorite that plays with the idea of a navy-type sub was:

Swiss missing
in one-ton sub

This flip and catchy idea came from D. Jones and J. Chamberlain at the Hall of Justice.

Sub to surface
on Swiss street

Moving on to the heroes, I liked Honeoye's Scott Woodruff's attempt:

A hero going
for a record

And while we're thinking hero, sub and torpedo we may as well throw in buns—and that rhymes with puns and we had a carload of them.

Jud Breslin of Rochester is a punster.

The only thing worse than his counts on headlines were the puns. Each seemingly worse than the last:

Swiss to make
a hambigger

Swiss idea is
much butter

Swiss knead 590
feet for record

Writing Summaries

SUMMARY EXERCISE 1

In order to write headlines, you have to understand the main idea of the story and then express its feeling, tone, or theme in seven words or less. Now that you understand how to condense information into a headline, you will work on condensing information to write a summary.

A summary is a shortened or condensed form of a piece of writing. It is used for a variety of purposes. You already use summary when you tell a shortened version of a story; a critic usually summarizes (or tells the plot of) a movie or play while offering his or her opinion. When students go to the library to do research, they condense the information for use later.

In this exercise, you will read an article and learn how to summarize it.

Read the article below. Then answer the questions that follow the article.

Business aims to pamper commuters

By Kathryn McKenzie Nichols

Gannett News Service

EMERYVILLE, Calif.—It's the typical California story: One day, in the middle of her 90-minute commute, Mable Yee wondered to herself:

What could be done to ease the plight of weekday road warriors?

Yee thought she could answer the question; thus was born Commuter Products Corp., perhaps the first company in the country to offer a mail-order catalog of commuter-care products.

Included is a $119.95 mini-refrigerator that plugs into the cigarette lighter. Flip a switch and it becomes a food warmer.

To guard against coffee splashes and croissant crumbs, Yee offers a $14.95 commuter apron. After a hard day, a driver can switch on a $79.95 seat pad with a heating element to ease lower back pain.

"I wanted to provide products and concepts to help people use their commute time productively," said Yee, who once worked in marketing and sales for Xerox Corp. "People tend to waste their commute time and zone out."

Yee, 37, used to spend three hours a day on Bay Area freeways. In February, she looked into the commuter product business, and the catalog appeared in November. Now she faces only a 15-minute drive to work.

Finding the items was not easy. Many products come from new, small companies that do not have the output to supply major stores, and she snapped up those items.

"We offer a lot of items for under $50," she said, adding that the most expensive item is the $1,595 portable fax machine and copier.

To receive a catalog or order items, call (415) 420-6660.

Comprehension Questions

1. What is a commuter?

____

2. What are commuter products?

____

3. Who sells them?

____

4. How did she get the idea?

____

5. Why does she sell commuter products?

____

6. Can you name some commuter products?

____

7. What's the main idea of the article?

   Who sells commuter products?
   What are some commuter products?

   Combine this information into one or two sentences.

____

A Sample Summary

Now think about how you might use the information from the article to write a summary. See how you can build a summary from important information, as in the sample done for you below.

1. What is the main idea in the article on page 64?	Mrs. Yee sells commuter products.
2. To expand on that, add more details.	She travels three hours a day by car.
3. Who is Mrs. Yee? (a lady who traveled three hours a day to work)	Mrs. Yee, a lady who traveled three hours a day to work, sells commuter products.

4. What products did she sell? (mini-refrigerator, fax machine, electric blanket)	Mrs. Yee, a lady who traveled three hours a day to work, sells commuter products such as mini-refrigerators, heating blankets, and fax machines.
5. Why does she sell these things?	She sells these things to make travel to work more pleasant.

Summary: Mrs. Yee, who used to travel to work three hours per day, got the idea to sell commuter products to make driving to and from work more pleasant. She now sells a mini-refrigerator that plugs into a cigarette lighter, a heating pad, an apron, a fax machine, and a food warmer.

SUMMARY EXERCISE 2

Read the article below. Then answer the questions that follow the article.

Teen-agers grab a crab to hang around their necks

By Lisa Perlman
The Associated Press

Monica Leeuwenburg with her pet hermit tree-crab and his pendant house.

GRAND RAPIDS, Mich.—Crabs for Christmas?

Sounds strange, but tiny hermit tree-crabs that teen-agers are buying as pets and wearing on chains around their necks may be one of the hot new gifts under, or perhaps climbing up, the tree this year.

"When they're on the person, it usually takes five or six minutes before he'll feel comfortable enough to come out of his shell and crawl around on the person's clothes," said James Allemon, owner of Indian Harbor, a Rockford gift shop that began selling the 1-inch Caribbean crabs in September.

He first sold the crabs, supplied by a Tennessee company, as pets in miniature terrariums. But when Allemon and his wife noticed loops on some of the crabs' gold-tone trimmed seashells, they decided the crustaceans would make the perfect pendant.

He's sold about 50 of the $6.95 crab necklaces—mostly to teen-agers—in the past two months and about 500 in cages.

Rockford High School sophomore Monica Leeuwenburg has only worn her crab, named Future, to school a couple of times. She knows a few other students who wear the crabs as necklaces and several more who keep them as pets.

"I think of him more as a pet than as jewelry, but I'll wear him every once in a while, like, when I go to the mall," said Leeuwenburg, 16. "You can't cuddle him or kiss him like a dog, but he's a lot of fun and a lot easier to take care of."

Assistant Principal Steven Lewis said the fad was news to him, and the school didn't have any standing policy regarding crustaceans in class.

Hermit crabs, including the tree-crab species, live in the empty shells of snails and similar gastropods for protection. They can live to be 70 years old.

But animal rights advocates aren't amused.

"We are against any unnecessary activity which may impede an animal's natural life," Ken Johnson, an investigator for the Humane Society of the United States, said from Washington.

Comprehension Questions

Use the answers to these questions to help you write a summary of the above article.

1. What is the article about? Write the main idea.

____

____

____

2. What pieces of information explain or prove the main idea?

____

____

____

3. To write your summary, combine your answers to questions 1 and 2.

____

____

____

Sentence Combining

One way to condense information is to combine sentences. To practice this important skill, complete the exercise below.

COMBINING EXERCISE

Combine the information in each of the groups of sentences into one sentence. The first one has been done for you.

Teenagers are buying hermit crabs. Teenagers are buying Christmas presents. Teenagers are buying pets.	Teenagers are buying hermit crabs as pets for Christmas.
Hermit crabs are popular. Hermit crabs are Christmas gifts.	______________________ ______________________
Teenagers wear hermit crabs. Teenagers wear hermit crabs on a chain. Teenagers wear hermit crabs around their necks.	______________________ ______________________ ______________________
Hermit crabs come out of their shells. It takes five or six minutes.	______________________ ______________________
Allemon sells hermit crabs. They cost $6.95. He has sold 50 of them as necklaces. Teenagers buy the crabs. He sold 500 of them in cages.	______________________ ______________________ ______________________ ______________________ ______________________

SUMMARY EXERCISE 3

In the spaces provided, list three movies that you have seen recently. Next to each title, write a summary explaining what the movie was about. Your teacher may choose to post these summaries on a bulletin board for class reference. This can become an ongoing class project in which the bulletin board is updated on a regular basis. Television shows can also be used.

1. ______________________________

____

____

2. ______________________________

____

____

3. ______________________________

____

____

SUMMARY EXERCISE 4

List three books that you have read, and in a few sentences tell what each book was about. Your teacher may post these summaries on a bulletin board for the class to use in determining what books to read.

1. ______________________________

____

____

2. ______________________________

____

____

3. ______________________________

____

____

SUMMARY EXERCISE 5

Read the article below. Answer the questions that follow the article, and then write a summary of no more than three sentences.

Picassos of pachydermia

Bruce Weber

Certain artists can be fairly described as heavy. [Take] Suti, for example. The 6,500-pound African elephant wielding her "brush" in the photograph above is one of three elephants at the Lincoln Park Zoo in Chicago, all of whom have exhibited an inclination toward, if not exactly a talent for, painting. (Suti's work is shown below left; below right, a distinctly different sample from Bozie, an Asian elephant.)

"In the wild, animals will spend most of their time foraging for food," says Dr. Lester E. Fisher, director of the zoo. "An elephant will spend a day just moving around eating. In captivity, we've restricted the size of their environment, so current zoo philosophy is to try and give them things to do.

We give climbing animals a place to climb, swimming animals a place to swim."

And painting animals?

"The painting is just another thing for them to do," Fisher says. "We have people who spend most of the day with the elephants, basically just to keep them occupied." Indeed, keepers often teach them small tricks—picking one leg up, for instance—or involve them in activities like dragging carts around by a harness, so that they're used to interacting with humans and can be managed easily when they need medical treatment.

Beyond that, Fisher says, "we're trying to make life interesting for them. Perhaps painting gives them pleasure. Who knows? But when they get the opportunity, they do it."

Actually, the Lincoln Park Zoo has a long history of artists. "We started with chimps in the children's zoo about 25 years ago," Fisher says. "I remember once one of the keepers in our great ape house gave a piece of heavy cardboard to Koundu"—a gorilla—"and tossed into the cage a whole bunch of crayons. The chimps used to let us have the finished drawings. Koundu ate his."

Summary Questions

1. What do the elephants do?

____

2. Where do they do it?

____

3. Why do they do it?

____

4. What else is important for the reader to know?

____

5. Write your summary in the space below.

____

____

____

____

____

SUMMARY EXERCISE 6

Choose an article from a newspaper or magazine. Read and summarize it.

Next, give the summary to a group of three or four students. Tell them to read it.

Give the original article to another group of three or four students, and ask them to write four questions about the article.

Give the four questions to the group with the summary.

Were they able to answer the questions? Why or why not?

Chapter 4

Writing Instructions

The goals for this chapter are:

To learn what's needed for a reader to follow instructions

To read clear instructions

To write clear instructions

To learn to use illustrations to help write instructions

- sequencing
- isolating the most important information
- thinking about the steps (brainstorming)
- learning to be precise

To learn to use illustrations to supplement instructions

When I was a young girl, I used to make chocolate cake with my grandmother. It was the best chocolate cake I have ever eaten. When I got older, I asked my grandmother for the recipe. Since she never measured anything, all she could say was "a little of this and a handful of that." I went home and tried to make that chocolate cake, but it was a disaster. The knife wouldn't even cut into the cake! What was the problem? Why did my cake fail?

When we give someone instructions, we must be precise. Instructions such as "a little" or "a handful" are very subjective. Different people interpret them differently. In addition, people have different size hands!

Have you ever had trouble following someone's directions? Why? What happened? Have you ever had trouble following the instructions to assemble or use something that you purchased at the store, such as a watch, calculator, bicycle, bookcase, etc.? Why? What happened?

In most cases, it is because the writer or speaker did not give you specific instructions. In this chapter, we will use our expertise in writing clear sentences to write directions for a variety of purposes. Writing instructions helps us to see what happens when our information isn't clear. By writing instructions and watching someone follow our instructions, we understand how the reader processes information. This helps us to become better writers.

Giving Written Instructions

To give clear written instructions, the writer must focus on the task and provide only that information which will help the person to do the task.

To do this well, you must be concise, to the point, and precise. There are four things that you must do.

1. All information should be relevant.
2. Information should be carefully organized in the correct order (sequence).
3. The instructions should be clear and easy to follow.
4. You should remember your audience. (You would write differently to your six-year-old sister than you would write to your teacher.)

GIVING WRITTEN INSTRUCTIONS EXERCISE 1

Look at the instructions below. There are one or two unnecessary steps. Find them and cross them out.

How to Polish Silver

1. Gather all the silver that you wish to polish.
2. Find a counter or table near the sink.

3. Assemble a cloth and some silver polish.
4. Dip the silverware into the silver polish.
5. If you have large pieces of silver, put some polish on a cloth and apply it to the silver.
6. Rinse with water.
7. Wipe dry.
8. Admire the silver.
9. Put the silver back where you store it.
10. Silver is truly beautiful when it has been polished.

GIVING WRITTEN INSTRUCTIONS EXERCISE 2

Think of something (a process or procedure) that you could give instructions for. List on a separate sheet of paper all the steps to complete the task. You could choose changing a light bulb, washing the floor, covering a book, and so forth. Then think of two or three steps that are related but that really don't have anything to do with completing the task, like admiring the silver in the previous exercise. Add these steps to your list. Then give the list to a classmate. Your classmate's task is to find the two or three items that are not relevant and cross them out.

GIVING WRITTEN INSTRUCTIONS EXERCISE 3

In the last exercise, we practiced using only important (relevant) information. In this exercise, we will practice putting the information in the correct order. The steps below describing how to do laundry are not in the right order. Read them and then renumber them correctly so that they will be in the correct order.

How to Do Laundry

1. Separate white clothes from colored clothes.
2. Collect quarters to pay for the machine.
3. Set the water temperature to hot for white clothes.
4. Add 1 cup of soap.
5. Add 1 cup of bleach for white clothes.
6. Put clothes into the washing machine.
7. Put clothes into the dryer.
8. Check labels inside clothes to make sure they can go into the dryer.
9. Put money into the washing machine.
10. Colored clothes can be washed in cold water.
11. Do not use bleach for colored clothes.
12. Check to be sure that all clothes are washable. Some may need to go to the dry cleaners.
13. Bring a book or homework with you so that you will have something to do while you wait for the clothes to be washed and dried.

GIVING WRITTEN INSTRUCTIONS EXERCISE 4

Here is an example of giving instructions on how to prune, trim, or cut leaves on a plant that is in a hanging basket.

Pruning hanging plants

Tovah Martin

Houseplants often need a haircut when sun becomes scant in midwinter. Hanging basket plants, in particular, tend to grow leggy when the days are short. Tradescantias, ivies, begonias and hanging geraniums all benefit from a shearing to rid them of straggly, sparsely foliated growth and to prepare them for spring's new flush of fresh foliage.

1. Bring down the basket to eye level and use a pair of sharp pruners to evenly cut all the old stems neatly around the rim of the pot, leaving only the new growth on the top.

2. At the same time, groom the top by cutting out any brown and dead branches. Leave only the short, new growth. While your plant is freshly shorn, check for any signs of insect infestations or disease. Often, mealy bugs hide in the tangle of a hanging plant's long locks.

3. It is difficult to repot a hanging basket plant when the foliage is draping over the container, so turn the plant upside down and check the root system now while the jungle is cleared away. If roots have completely filled the pot, give the plant a new container. In a month's time, your plant will be on the road to looking lush and full again.

Notice how the illustrations help the reader to understand the instructions. Then answer the questions that follow the illustrations.

Comprehension Questions

1. What is the very first thing the writer tells the reader to do?

____

2. What is the next step?

____

3. Do the illustrations help you to understand the instructions? How?

____

4. What does "to prune" mean? What are pruners?

____

5. What should be left when you are finished trimming the plant?

____

6. Besides trimming the old stems, what else should be removed?

____

7. In addition to cutting the plant, what else should you be doing?

____

8. Besides trimming the plant, what else does the writer tell you to do?

____

9. When is it a good idea to give a plant a new pot?

____

10. How long will it take for the plant to look full again?

____

GIVING WRITTEN INSTRUCTIONS EXERCISE 5

When you write instructions, it is important to explain each step in the process.

Look at the illustrations and captions below that explain how to clean a paintbrush and roller. Notice how the captions explain each step in the process. Then answer the questions that follow the illustrations.

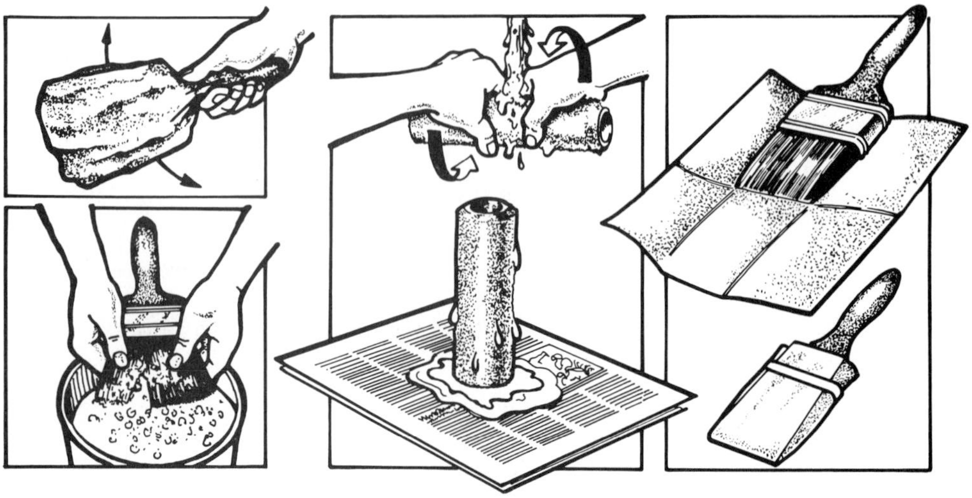

Clean between the brush bristles, especially at the top. Dry brush best by shaking it in a bag.

To clean a roller, wring gently while washing it. Raise nap by rubbing. Stand it on end to dry.

To store a brush, put it on a flat sheet cut from a paper bag. Then secure sheet with a rubber band.

Discussion Questions

1. How should a paintbrush be cleaned?
2. What part of the paintbrush is especially important to clean?
3. What is the best way to dry a paintbrush? What do you think is the reason or logic behind this method?
4. When cleaning a roller, what two things can you do simultaneously?
5. How should a roller be dried?
6. How should a paintbrush be stored?
7. What questions do you, the reader, have? Are there some things that you wish the writer had told you? What are they?

Analyzing Written Instructions

Now read the article that the newspaper printed with the pictures and captions on how to clean a paintbrush and roller. Notice how the article expands upon the information that was illustrated. Then answer the questions below and on page 80.

Discussion Questions

1. Does the article answer any of the questions you had after looking at the illustrations?
2. What does the first sentence tell the reader?
3. What information about washing paintbrushes is in the article that wasn't in the illustrations?

Home improvement The proper care of rollers and paintbrushes

John Warde

To clean both brushes and rollers, first wipe them between layers of newspaper to remove as much residue as possible. Wash brushes used with water-based material under warm running water. Rinse with clear water. Clean between the bristles, especially at the top where they join the handle.

When the brush is clean, insert it up to the handle in a plastic or paper bag, close the top by gripping it around the handle, and shake the brush to dry it without creating a mess. Smooth and shape the cleaned bristles so they lie flat, square the edges and tip and then lay the brush flat on newspaper or suspend it by the handle to dry completely.

To clean a roller used with water-based materials, remove it from the handle and wash it as described. It helps to wring the roller with your hands during washing, but be careful not to crush the core.

When the roller is clean, rub it to raise the nap, then stand it upright on newspaper to dry. Do not lay a damp roller flat or it will develop a flat spot. Clean the handle with soapy water.

To clean brushes or rollers used with solvent-based materials, different techniques are required. For brushes, fill a wide-mouthed can or jar with about an inch of the appropriate solvent. Turpentine or mineral spirits are standard solvents for paint, varnish and stain; lacquer thinner is the solvent for lacquer, and denatured alcohol is the solvent for shellac. Emulsifying cleaners for brushes and rollers are also available that allow washing the item clean with soap and water, sometimes without using solvent beforehand.

Press the bristles of the brush against the base of the can or jar and flex them vigorously in the solvent or cleaner several times, until the liquid becomes saturated with residue. Then pour the liquid into a container for disposal and replace it with a fresh supply. Wipe the brush on clean newspapers. Repeat the process.

Continue wiping until the brush no longer produces streaks of color. Then wash the brush in a small amount of warm soapy water and rinse it with clear water. Shake the brush as dry as possible inside a bag as previously described, then smooth the bristles, shape the edges and lay the brush flat or hang it vertically by the handle to dry completely.

If you choose to clean a roller used with solvent-based material, put on disposable rubber gloves or insert your hands into plastic food storage bags to protect them. Remove the roller from the handle and place it in a clean roller tray; then pour on an inch or so of solvent or cleaner. Gently squeeze and wring out the cover in the liquid, then wipe it on newspaper.

Replace the dirty solvent or cleaner with a fresh amount and repeat the process. When the roller is clean, wash it briefly in warm soapy water, rinse it in clear water, and stand it on end to dry. Clean the roller handle with a cloth dipped in solvent.

Brushes and rollers should be wrapped before being put away. To wrap a brush, cut a paper bag into a flat sheet and fold it around the bristles. Secure the wrapping with a rubber band, but do not crimp the bristles. Rollers can be placed in paper or perforated plastic bags. There should be some air circulation to prevent mildew.

Reprinted, by permission, from *The New York Times* (December 6, 1990).

4. After the brush is clean, how should it be dried?
5. What information about drying brushes is in the article but not in the illustrations?
6. How should rollers be cleaned?
7. What information about cleaning rollers was not illustrated?
8. After the roller is clean, how should it be dried?
9. What information about drying rollers is in the article but not in the illustrations?
10. Why do you think the article is different from the illustrations in these ways?
11. Could the illustrations have had all of the information found in the article? Would they have been effective?
12. Look at the article and the instructions. What words are used to tell the reader the order in which things should be done? Can you think of any other words that you could use?

GIVING WRITTEN INSTRUCTIONS EXERCISE 6

Think of written instructions that you could give to someone on how to do or make something. For example, you might choose instructions on how to play a game, cover a book, make a paper airplane, or frame a picture. Choose something that you know very well and that will not be complicated to explain. Below are some ideas to help you plan your instructions.

Planning

1. Decide what you will write instructions for. Write your topic here.

___

2. List the tools, materials, or things a person would need to complete the task.

___

3. In the space below, draw a rough sketch of the most important steps that someone will have to do to follow your instructions.

4. Check that your sketches are in the correct order. If they are not in the right order, number them correctly, or photocopy them, cut them out, and paste them below in the correct order. (You may also redraw them if you wish.)

5. Write a caption for each sketch.

____

____

6. Write one or two sentences that tell the reader what the instructions will help the reader do or make.

____

____

7. Compare your sketches with the materials you listed in number 2 above. Have you forgotten to mention anything?

____

8. Which of these connecting words and phrases will help the reader understand the order in which to do things?

first	after that
second	when you have done that
next	finally
then	

____

9. Using your sketches and captions as a guide, have a classmate follow your instructions as you tell him or her what to do. Write down any questions your classmate asks so that you can use them to improve your instructions.

____

____

10. Make changes in the sketches and captions based on your experience in step number 9.

____

____

Writing Your Instructions

Now write out your instructions. Be sure to tell the reader in the first one or two sentences what the instructions are for. Then use the captions and finished sketches as a guide as you develop your written instructions. Use appropriate connecting words to tell the reader the order in which to do things. Remember, you can add some additional information here if you wish. Whatever information you add must be relevant to the instructions.

Following Up

1. Bring to class the materials needed to follow your instructions.
2. Exchange materials and instructions with another classmate. (Do not give them to the same classmate who went over your work before.) Each of you should follow each other's instructions and complete the project.
3. As you follow the instructions, write down any questions you have. Also write down any suggestions you have on how your classmate can improve the instructions.

GIVING WRITTEN INSTRUCTIONS EXERCISE 7

Writing Recipes

Recipes are another form of giving instructions. Recipes tell someone how to cook or prepare a specific food. Look at the recipes below. What do they have in common? What kinds of vocabulary words are used in recipes? After you have looked at the recipes below, answer the questions that follow these recipes.

Infused oils

Flavored oils, more healthful than cream- or butter-based sauces and dressings, also can replace salt as a food seasoning. Make infused oils using any dried herb or spice, such as curry, nutmeg or cloves, and light oils, particularly canola, safflower and sunflower.

1. Mix 1 tablespoon of herb or spice with water to make a thick paste. (Amount of water needed will vary depending on spice used.)

2. Pour 1 cup oil and paste into a jar and shake. Let stand at room temperature to allow flavors to infuse the oil.

3. After three days, ladle the infused oil into a jar and discard the paste that has separated. Cover and store oil in the refrigerator for up to six months.

Reprinted, by permission, from *Organic Gardening* (January 1991), 25.

RECIPE FOR MOM'S BEEF STEW

Ingredients

2 pounds beef, cut in cubes
¼ cup ketchup
2 12-ounce cans ginger ale
1 envelope dried onion soup

Instructions
Put ketchup, ginger ale, and onion soup in a heavy pot. Heat over medium heat. Add beef and stir until beef is covered with sauce. Cover and cook for 1½ hours. Serves 6 people.

Discussion Questions

1. How much beef should you use in the recipe for beef stew?
2. How many people will the recipe for beef stew feed?
3. What units of measurement do you need to know to follow an American recipe?

Recipe Writing Guidelines

1. Give the ingredients first.
2. Tell how much of each of the ingredients is needed.
3. Tell the order in which to use the ingredients.
4. Explain how to combine the ingredients: use words such as *mix, stir, beat, pour,* etc.
5. Use action verbs that apply to cooking: *mix, heat, bake, broil, boil, fry, add, shake, pour, beat, stir.*
6. Tell what the temperature of the oven should be or how high the heat should be on the stove.
7. Tell how many people the recipe serves.
8. Tell how long the food must cook.

Recipe Exercise 1: The class should choose a recipe that can be done in class. As a class, write out the instructions and then follow them in class. Some suggestions are to make popcorn, sandwiches (either meat and cheese or peanut butter and jelly), or salads. If someone can bring in an electric frying pan, the class can make French toast, scrambled eggs, or omelettes.

After you have completed the task, discuss what made it easy or difficult to follow the instructions.

Recipe Exercise 2: On a separate sheet of paper, write a recipe for your favorite dish.

Recipe Exercise 3: Exchange recipes with a classmate. Each of you should go home and try the new recipe. Bring in a sample of the dish, if possible, for your classmate to taste. Does your classmate think it tastes the same as when he or she prepares it at home?

If you can't actually prepare the dish, read the recipe and write down any questions you may have. It is important for the writer to know what kinds of questions his or her audience may have.

Explaining How Things Work

Explaining how something works is similar to writing instructions for someone to follow. The major difference is that the person writing an explanation understands how the subject works but either cannot or is not expected to make it happen. For example, someone can explain how the moon controls the tide, or how the earth revolves around the sun, but he or she is not expected to make either of these things happen!

EXPLAINING HOW THINGS WORK EXERCISE 1

On the next page is a scientific explanation of how oxbows (bends or loops made by a river) are formed.

Look at the illustrations and read the captions. Then answer the questions that follow the illustrations.

River's loops fit to be tied? How an oxbow is formed

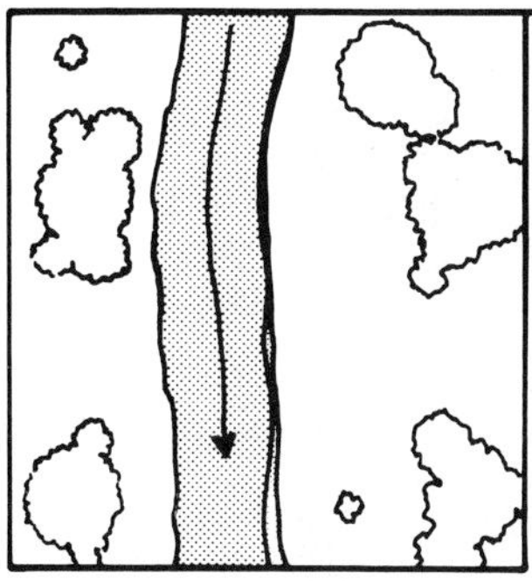

Starts with a straight channel of a river.

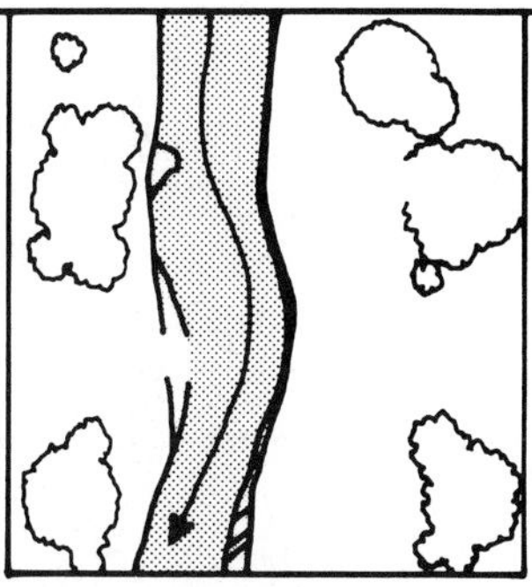

Starts to cut into a bank, eroding one side and building up deposits on the other.

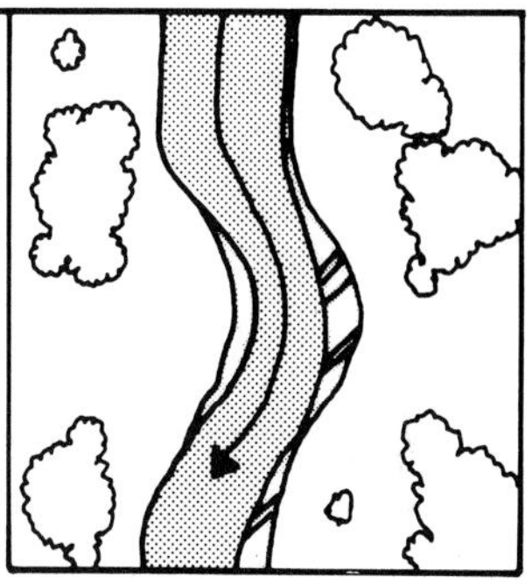

Erosion continues to eat into the land, while the deposits opposite the point of erosion also continue to build.

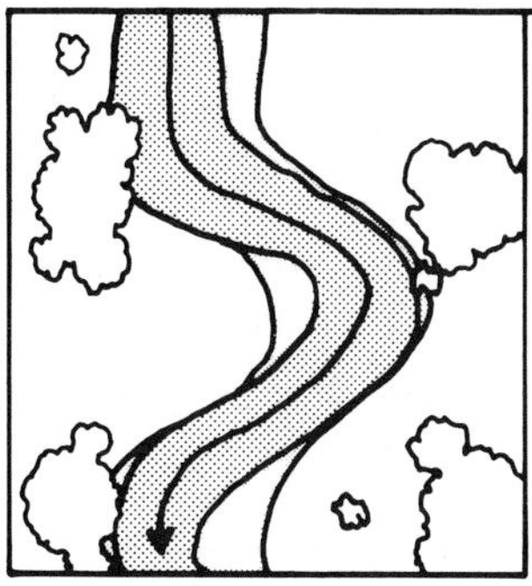

Curves or meanders develop, further eroding the banks.

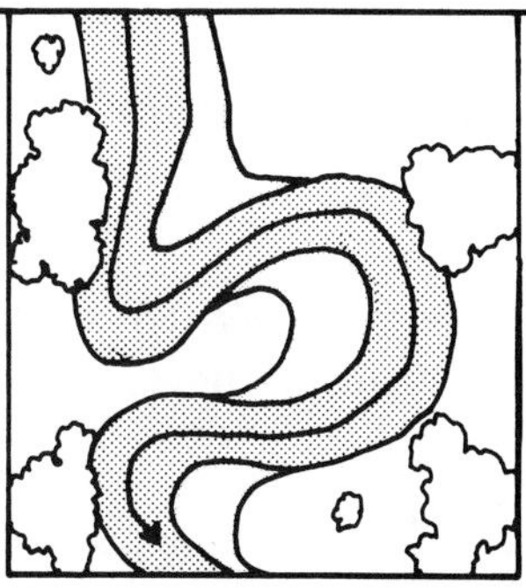

The three curves enlarge in all directions along their peripheries.

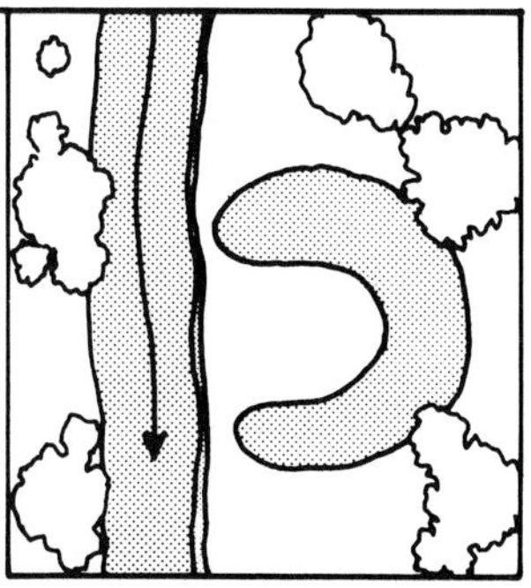

The upper and lower curves meet, straightening the stream and leaving the oxbow isolated as a pond or lake.

Discussion Questions

1. Before an oxbow is formed, is the river straight?
2. What begins to happen to the river?
3. What is erosion?
4. While one side of a riverbank is eroded, what happens on the other side?
5. What finally happens to the river?

Look at the picture below.

South Alligator Riv. on Arnhem Land, near Darwin, No. Territory Australia

1. What is an oxbow like?
2. How could you make one if you wanted to?
3. Is an oxbow a good natural phenomenon? Why or why not?

EXPLAINING HOW THINGS WORK EXERCISE 2

Below are a number of short explanations and diagrams that show how light works and images form. Read the explanations. Notice that very few words are used to explain each process. How are the diagrams used to supplement the text? Do they help you understand the process being explained?

LIGHT RAYS

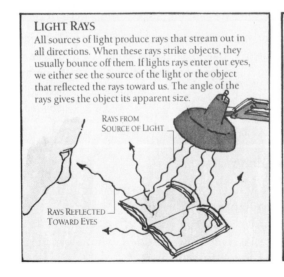

All sources of light produce rays that stream out in all directions. When these rays strike objects, they usually bounce off them. If lights rays enter our eyes, we either see the source of the light or the object that reflected the rays toward us. The angle of the rays gives the object its apparent size.

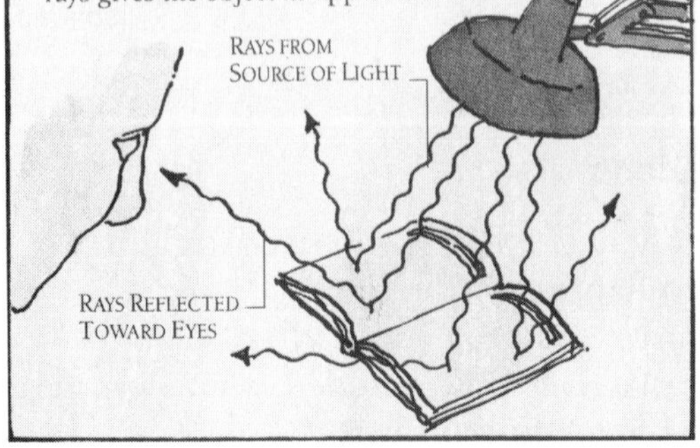

EYESIGHT

The lens of the eye bends the light rays that come from an object. It forms an image of the object on the light-sensitive retina of the eye, and this image is then changed to nerve impulses which travel to the brain. The image is in fact upside down on the retina, but the brain interprets it as upright.

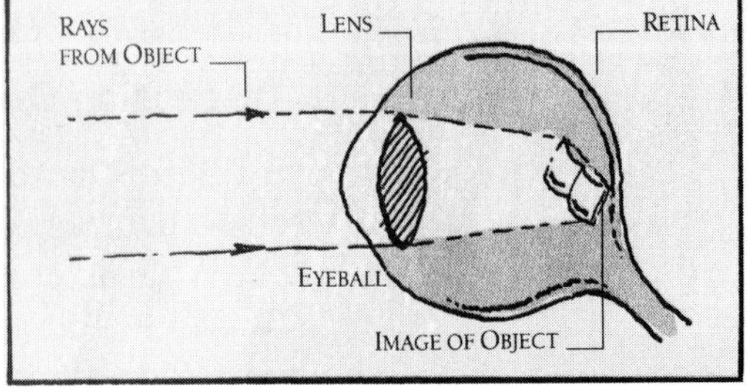

Reprinted, by permission, from *The Way Things Work,* 190–193.

Reprinted, by permission, from *The Way Things Work,* 190–193.

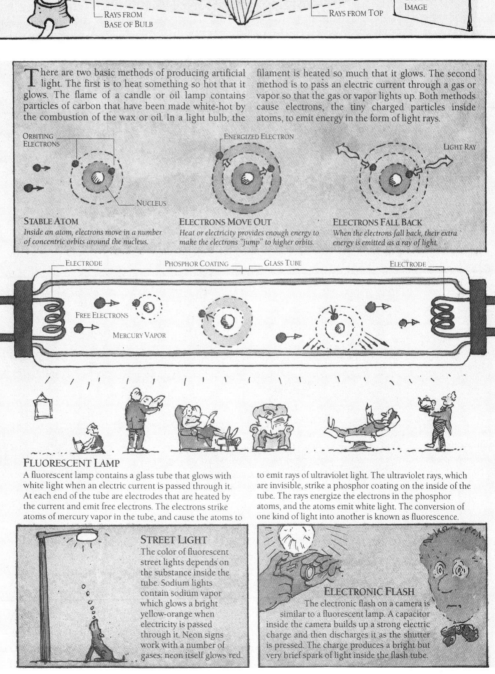

FORMING IMAGES

As light rays enter and leave transparent materials such as glass, they bend or refract. Seen through a lens, a nearby object appears to be much bigger because the rays enter the eye in a wider angle than they would without it. This is why the mammoth's eye is magnified by the discus.

Lenses can also throw images onto a surface. Cones of rays from every point on the object are bent by the lens to meet at the surface. The cones cross, inverting the mammoths, while the sun's rays meet to form a hot spot on the wall.

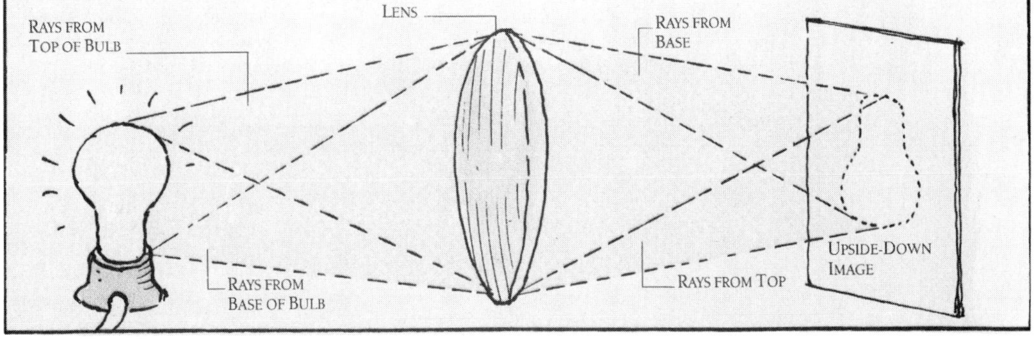

There are two basic methods of producing artificial light. The first is to heat something so hot that it glows. The flame of a candle or oil lamp contains particles of carbon that have been made white-hot by the combustion of the wax or oil. In a light bulb, the filament is heated so much that it glows. The second method is to pass an electric current through a gas or vapor so that the gas or vapor lights up. Both methods cause electrons, the tiny charged particles inside atoms, to emit energy in the form of light rays.

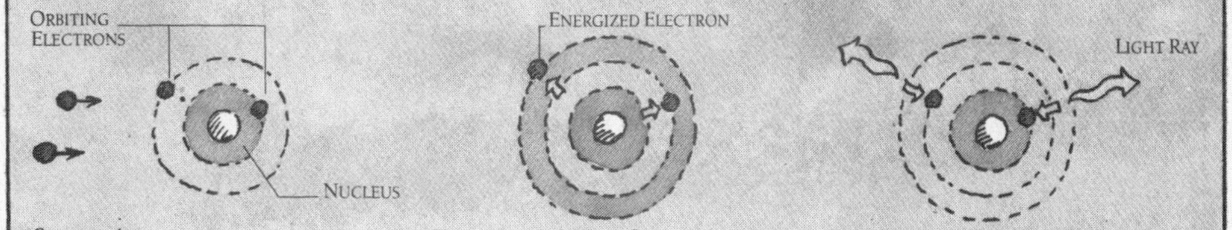

STABLE ATOM
Inside an atom, electrons move in a number of concentric orbits around the nucleus.

ELECTRONS MOVE OUT
Heat or electricity provides enough energy to make the electrons "jump" to higher orbits.

ELECTRONS FALL BACK
When the electrons fall back, their extra energy is emitted as a ray of light.

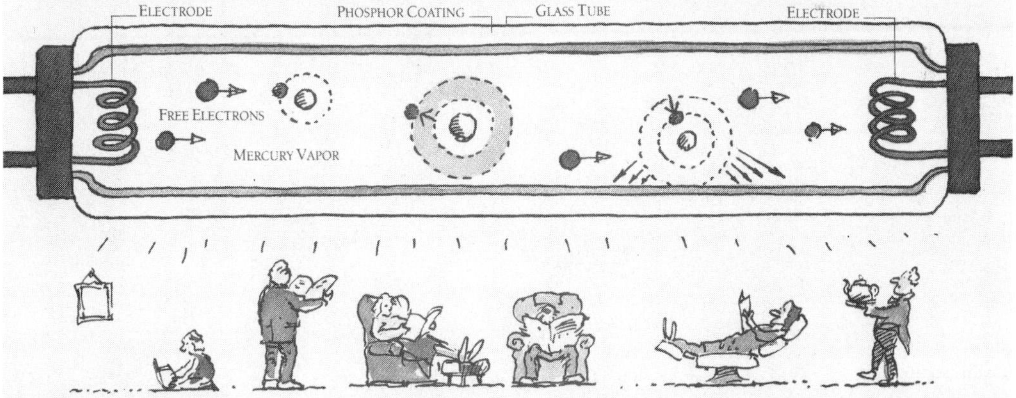

FLUORESCENT LAMP

A fluorescent lamp contains a glass tube that glows with white light when an electric current is passed through it. At each end of the tube are electrodes that are heated by the current and emit free electrons. The electrons strike atoms of mercury vapor in the tube, and cause the atoms to emit rays of ultraviolet light. The ultraviolet rays, which are invisible, strike a phosphor coating on the inside of the tube. The rays energize the electrons in the phosphor atoms, and the atoms emit white light. The conversion of one kind of light into another is known as fluorescence.

STREET LIGHT
The color of fluorescent street lights depends on the substance inside the tube. Sodium lights contain sodium vapor which glows a bright yellow-orange when electricity is passed through it. Neon signs work with a number of gases: neon itself glows red.

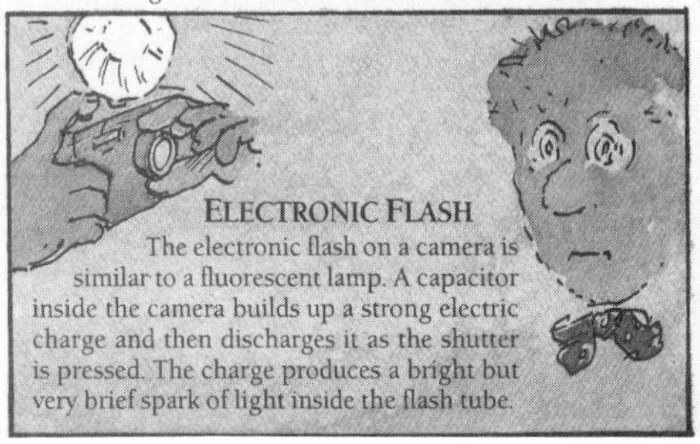

ELECTRONIC FLASH
The electronic flash on a camera is similar to a fluorescent lamp. A capacitor inside the camera builds up a strong electric charge and then discharges it as the shutter is pressed. The charge produces a bright but very brief spark of light inside the flash tube.

Reprinted, by permission, from *The Way Things Work,* 190–193.

LIGHT BULB

An electric light bulb consists of a filament of tungsten wire wound in a tight coil. The passage of electricity through the filament heats the coil so that it becomes white hot. The filament reaches a temperature of about 4,500°F (2,500°C). Tungsten is chosen because it has a very high melting point and will not melt as it heats up. The bulb contains an inert gas such as argon to prevent the metal combining with oxygen in the air, which would cause the filament to burn out. The gas is usually under reduced pressure.

In modern light bulbs each coil of the filament is often made up of even tinier coils. The filament is therefore very long but very thin. This arrangement increases its light output.

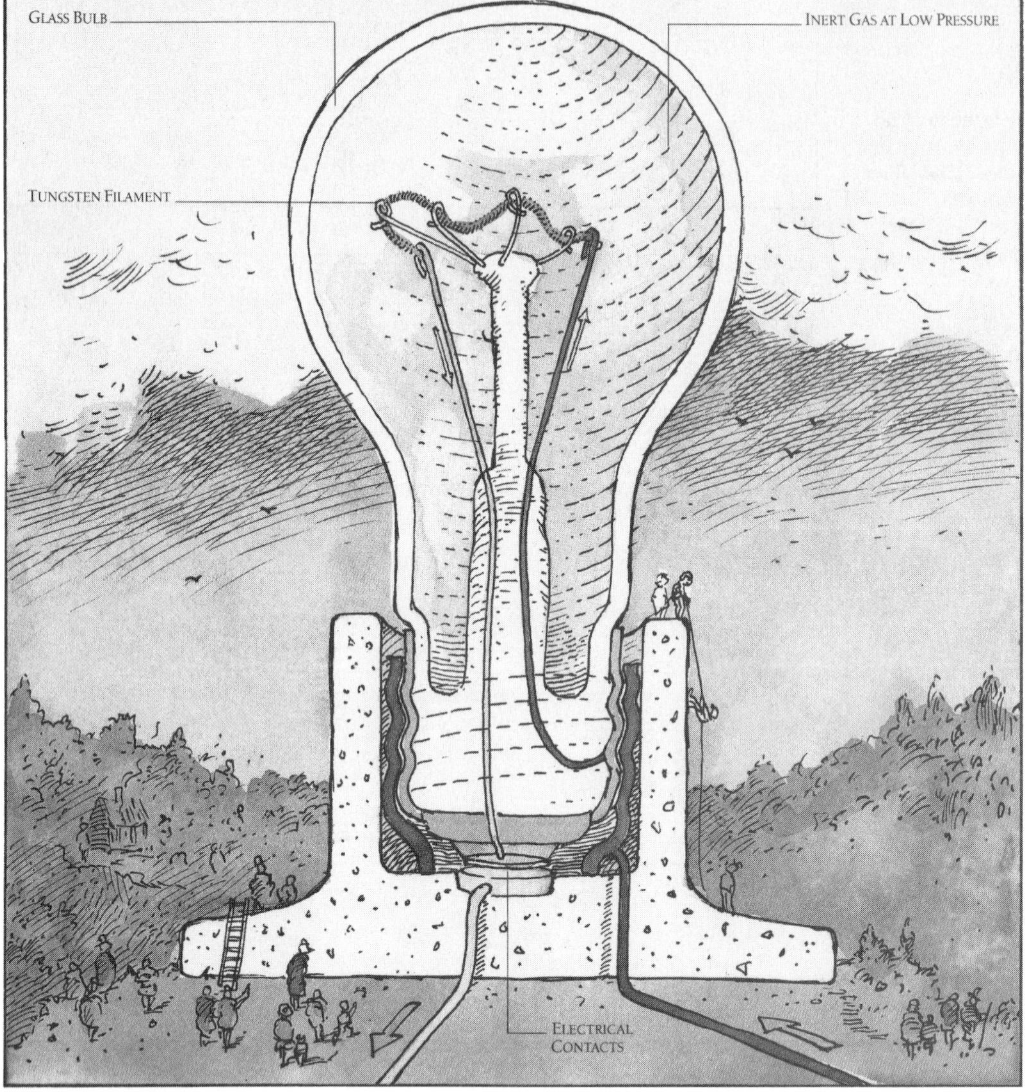

Reprinted, by permission, from *The Way Things Work,* 190–193.

EXPLAINING HOW THINGS WORK EXERCISE 3

Think of a subject that you can explain. Choose something simple. It could be how rain changes to snow, where rain comes from, how the heart or lungs work, why the sun rises in the morning and sets at night, and so forth. Be sure to choose something that you understand well.

Planning

1. What subject will you explain? Do you know enough about it to explain it to someone else? Who will your audience be?

2. What happens in the process, or how does it work?

3. Draw a simple sketch of each step in the process.

4. Be sure the steps are in the right order.

5. Write a caption under each sketch.

6. Have you omitted any of the steps in the process?

7. What connecting words will you use? Add them to the captions to connect the information in the sketches.

8. Are there any vocabulary words that you need to look up in the dictionary? Will your reader know the meaning of these words? If not, you must explain them.

Writing Your Explanation

After you have completed the above steps, write a short explanation of the subject you have chosen.

Chapter 5

Writing Descriptions

NYT Pictures

The goals for this chapter are:

To learn to use descriptive words

To distinguish between main ideas and supporting information

To read and analyze descriptive writing

To write descriptions

What is different about the three rooms shown below? What is the same about them? If you said that the basic form of each room is the same, but two of the drawings give the viewer more detail, you are correct. Let's analyze the drawings a little more closely.

1. What do drawings B and C have that drawing A doesn't have?
2. How are drawings B and C different from each other?

In this chapter we will study how to enrich writing so that the reader can learn more information from what is written.

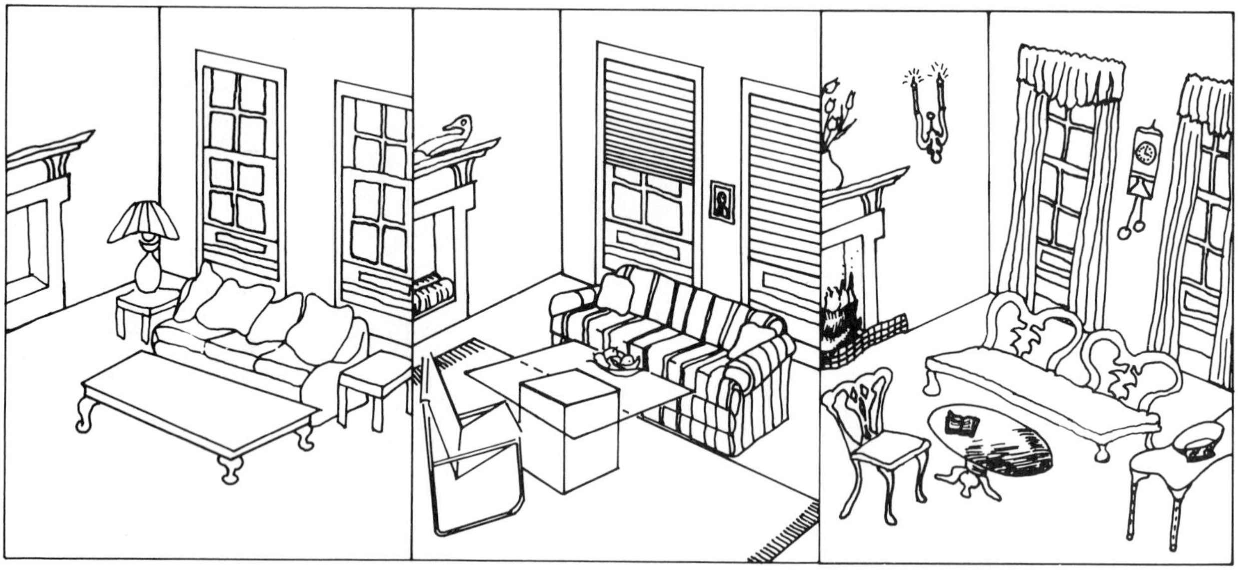

A B C

DESCRIPTIONS

In the United States, baseball hats are popular among kids of all ages. Usually they have the name or insignia of the wearer's favorite team. For example, a hat might say "Mets" for the New York Mets or "A's" for the Kansas City Athletics.

ANALYZING DESCRIPTIONS EXERCISE 1

Recently, a baseball hat with an unusual design appeared in New York City and was written about in the fashion section of *The New York Times.* Look at the pictures and read the short paragraph that describes these hats. Then answer the questions that follow the article.

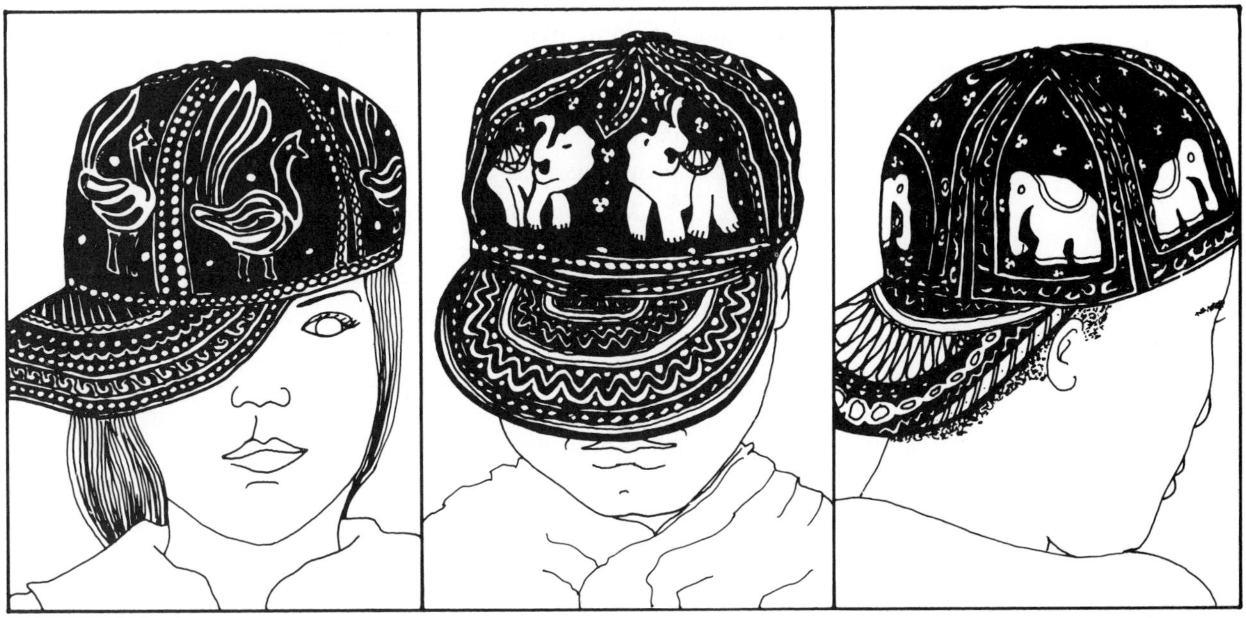

On the street

Put it on, play ball or tune in

With the World Series only two days away, it seems appropriate that at this moment a very hot fashion item is the baseball cap, though one with a difference.

Instead of insignias of Major League ball clubs, this one has such figures as elephants or exotic birds embroidered in gold thread, along with intricate patterns stitched into the bill and along the seams in the crown. Rather than polyester, it's made of black velvet.

In the best street-style tradition, this opulent-looking cap is worn many ways, with the bill frontward, backward or off to one side.

The cap, made in Thailand, is available from street vendors from Fifth Avenue in midtown to lower Broadway. The usual asking price is about $35.

Reprinted, by permission, from *The New York Times* (October 14, 1990), 49.

Discussion Questions

1. According to the short article, what is only two days away?

____

2. What is the World Series?

____

3. How is the hat different from other baseball hats?

____

4. How do people wear this hat? Name three ways.

____

5. Where is the hat made?

____

6. Who sells the hat? Where do they sell it?

____

7. How much does it cost?

____

8. Would you buy this hat? Why? Why not?

____

Paragraph Analysis

Notice how much information appears in three or four short paragraphs. Now let's consider the structure of the paragraph.

1. Read the first sentence in the article on unusual baseball hats. What is its purpose?
2. What information does the first sentence provide?
3. How does the author introduce the topic?
4. What information is provided in the third paragraph?
5. Is there any information that is new or different?
6. How is the hat in the article different from other baseball hats?
7. What words does the author use to describe the hat?
8. What sentence tells us what this short essay will be about?
9. What information demonstrates, proves, or supports the information in this sentence?

ANALYZING DESCRIPTIONS EXERCISE 2

The next article talks about another piece of clothing that is becoming popular in New York City. Read the short article that describes it. Look at the pictures, and then answer the questions that follow the article.

On the street
Call it fashion, American style

Fashion and patriotism often merge and this is one of those times. The American flag is now appearing frequently in the form of the newest leather jacket. White stars are embroidered on a navy leather background and white and red stripes are set into the back of a navy-blue leather jacket. This winter's design is from North Beach Leather. It's by Michael Hoban, who created leather jackets last year emblazoned with highway signs on the backs and elbows. Some bore numbers.

The original $800 designs have been widely copied by lower-priced manufacturers who use less-expensive leather and applique to replace the craftsmanship found in the original designs. After the war with Iraq began, North Beach Leather's Madison Avenue shop reported brisk flag-jacket sales to men, women and children.

Reprinted, by permission, from *The New York Times* (January 20, 1991), 37.

Discussion Questions

1. What are the jackets discussed in the article made of?
2. What design appears on these jackets?
3. Who is the designer?
4. What pattern did this designer put on jackets last year?
5. How much did the original jackets cost?
6. What is different about the less expensive jackets?
7. Why does the writer think these jackets with American flags became so popular?

Writing a Descriptive Essay

The first paragraph of an essay introduces the reader to the topic.

- The first sentence in the paragraph usually gets the reader interested and motivates the reader to want to read the rest of the essay.
- The rest of the paragraph may give the reader some background information. One way to help you think of what information to include is to ask yourself these questions:

Who?	Where?
What?	Why?
When?	How?

- One sentence in the paragraph usually tells the reader the main idea or purpose of the essay.

Each paragraph after that gives the reader information to prove or support the main idea that was stated in the first paragraph.

The last paragraph is called the conclusion. It is the ending to the essay. In it the writer can summarize the ideas expressed in the essay, ask questions that deal with this issue, or propose changes.

WRITING DESCRIPTIONS EXERCISE 1

Choose an article of clothing that is special in your country or in your family. Close your eyes and picture it carefully. Remember the color, the shape, the design. Turn it around in your mind so that you can see it from different angles. Then briefly write some notes here.

Be sure to explain its importance. Provide background information for a reader who may be unfamiliar with it. Tell when it is worn, by whom, etc. The questions below will guide you to write an essay in which you describe this article of clothing. Be sure to answer the questions before you begin writing your essay.

As you draft your essay, follow the guide questions below.

Guide Questions

1. In what country or countries do people wear it?
2. What is it?
3. What is it called?
4. How is it used?
5. What colors does it come in? Do the colors have special meanings?
6. When do people wear it?
7. What does it look like?
8. What is it made of?
9. Who usually wears it? Men, women, boys, girls, small children, teenagers?
10. Does it have a special meaning?

11. Does it have an interesting history? If so, what is its history?
12. How much does it cost?
13. Where can people buy it?
14. Does it come in different sizes?
15. Where is it made?

Organizational Questions

Now that you know the content you wish to include in your essay, you must consider how you will organize the essay. Use the questions below to guide the organization of your essay.

1. What is the purpose or main idea of your essay? Write your answer in a complete sentence.

____

2. What information do you want the reader to learn about this article of clothing? Write your answers in the left-hand column below.

Information	*Support*
a. ______________________	______________________
b. ______________________	______________________
c. ______________________	______________________

3. How can you elaborate on each of these ideas? In the right-hand column above, write how you will demonstrate each idea.

4. In what order do you want to present these ideas? Which one do you think you should talk about first? Second? Third? Number them.

5. What final statement or question would you like to make? It can be a statement or a question that you would like the reader to think about. This statement or question can be used as the last sentence of your essay.

____

6. Look at all the things you wrote above. What do you think will be a good way to get the reader interested in what you have to say? Write one sentence here. It can be a question, a statement, a quote, etc. This sentence will become your introductory sentence.

____

Writing Your Descriptive Essay

Now write the first paragraph of your essay in the space provided below, and complete it on a separate sheet of paper.

WRITING DESCRIPTIONS EXERCISE 2

Now you are ready to write a descriptive essay that requires you to pay attention to time sequence. In this assignment, you will use a series of photographs to describe in words the demolition of a building.

In 1980 an eighty-six-year-old building in Rochester, New York (the Commerce Building), was blown up to make room for a new building. Many people who wanted to watch the building be demolished came downtown on a cold, rainy day in order to watch.

On the next two pages is a *photo story* or *photo essay* of the demolition of the building. Look at the photographs and you will see what the photographers at the site saw that cold, wet morning. Read the caption under the first picture, and notice how the photographer tried to interpret the picture for the reader.

Photo Essay: Caption Analysis

One way to become more concise and still be descriptive is to analyze captions. The few sentences under pictures explain a great deal to the reader.

Look at the captions carefully.

1. Look at the caption under the first picture. What does this caption tell us? What is a "big boom"? What does David have drawn on his hat? What do you think his hat is made of?

____

2. What kind of attitude do you think David had about the building being demolished?

____

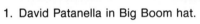

1. David Patanella in Big Boom hat.

2.

3.

4.

5. Commerce Building, seen from Holiday Inn 10th floor, collapses into cloud of chocolate-colored dust.

6. Nothing but a fairly neat pile of sticks remained when dust settled.

3. Look at photo numbers 5 and 6 and read the captions. What do the captions tell us?

---

4. Now write captions for photo numbers 2, 3, and 4.

---

5. We said the series of photos was a photo essay. Look at the pictures again.

   How is the first photo like an introduction?
   What do the other photos (2, 3, 4, and 5) tell us?
   How is the last photo like a conclusion? What does it tell the reader?

ANALYZING DESCRIPTIONS EXERCISE 3

The short article below summarized what happened at the Commerce Building. This article accompanied the photographs. Read the article and answer the questions that follow.

Last gasp

The long wait ended with a muffled explosion, then a deep-throated groan. Ornate cornices cracked, sliding earthward as 86 years of Rochester history collapsed into so much rubble. The Commerce Building died with dignity yesterday—after a cold, wet vigil for those who came to watch. It exhaled dust in a vast cloud, to settle on city streets. Onlookers cheered. Three hundred pounds of dynamite detonated from across the street atop the Genesee Plaza/Holiday Inn garage reduced the 13-story building to mere memories and photographs. The $40 million Rockefeller Center office-convention center project is a possibility for the site. And now, the cleanup. Full page of stories, photos on Page 3A.

Reprinted with permission from the *Times-Union* and *Democrat and Chronicle*, Rochester, NY (November 10, 1980).

Discussion Questions

1. What is the author's intent?
2. Why did the writer choose the headline "Last Gasp"?
3. What sounds did people hear?
4. What parts of the destroyed building does the writer describe?
5. How does the writer indicate that people waited a long time to watch the building be destroyed?
6. How tall was the building?
7. How much dynamite was used?
8. What may replace the building?

9. How did spectators react when the building came down?
10. What colorful words does the writer use so that the reader can "see" the building come down?
11. What colorful words does the writer use so that the reader can "hear" the sounds in the street?

ANALYZING DESCRIPTIONS EXERCISE 4

The article below accompanied the photo essay and the summary paragraph. It gives the reader a more complete picture of what happened. Read the article and then answer the questions that follow.

The first act dragged, but what a finale:
11-second kaboom dispatched Commerce Building

By Dede Murphy
D&C Staff Writer

Crowds waited on downtown bridges and sidewalks yesterday for almost five hours in the dark, the rain and the windy cold.

They were waiting for 11 quick seconds of noise and dust as 300 pounds of dynamite reduced the Commerce Building to rubble.

The 13-story building at East Main Street and South Avenue received cheers and a standing ovation from the wet, cold crowd of a few hundred as it finally sank into dust around 11 a.m. yesterday—four hours behind schedule.

At the detonation site across the street from the building, ABC Demolition and Xplo Corp. workers waved and took bows after the clouds of dust settled around the rubble. ABC of Arlington, Va., prime contractor for the demolition, will work for about a month clearing the site.

The day's saga began around 6 a.m. for most spectators, although workers had been on site since 1 a.m. placing the explosives. It was still dark and the ground was wet from a light rain when crowds began assembling.

Almost everyone had a camera. Many came equipped with folding chairs and coffee. A few campers were even parked at the curb on the Broad Street bridge. Inside, occupants were frying eggs for breakfast. Outside, people clustered together on the bridge to keep warm.

"Nothing ever happens in Rochester," said Al Ward, a Rochesterian who showed up on the bridge around 3 a.m. to make sure he got a good spot. "I always watch the buildings come down, so I figured I'd watch this one get blown down."

Larry Newell, a photojournalist from Johnson City, Tenn., happened to be in the area and heard about the demolition. So he packed up his cameras and parked his camper on the bridge.

"It looks good in your portfolio," he said. "Besides, we like the fireworks. Where I live, we had a streetlight burn out once and had a big party. Must have been a 100 people there."

"Strange group," a woman remarked, gliding past on rollerskates.

By 6:30 a.m., the sky was lightening, the clouds were clearing and the crowd on the bridge was larger. Demolition was scheduled for between 7 and 9 a.m. The police cars blocking streets around the building would sound their sirens 10 minutes before the blast to alert everyone.

At 7 a.m., the sky was clear. Cameras were poised. The crowd of about 3,000 was silent, everyone's eyes trained on the 13 stories of brick and concrete across the river.

Nothing happened.

Xplo workers could still be seen around the building, checking explosives and circuits.

In the Rochester Suite on the 14th floor of the Genesee Plaza/Holiday Inn, ABC Demolition had been having an early morning party while workers placed the explosives across the street.

Paul Haddad, head of ABC, was downstairs at the police-guarded detonation site. In the suite, friends and associates of ABC said detonation had been set for 8:30 a.m. But no one told the crowd outside, still staring at the building.

At 8 a.m., it started to get cloudy again. The crowds were still staring wistfully at the Commerce Building. On St. Paul Street, behind the Holiday Inn, the crowd was getting impatient. The conversation was occasionally punctuated by a shout to "Blow it" or "Drop it."

At 8:20, it began to rain. Suddenly, a chorus of police sirens cut through downtown, announcing the blast would be triggered in 10 minutes. "This is it, this is it," people begin telling each other, getting their cameras into position.

But it wasn't it.

At the detonation site, workers had tested the electrical circuits and found a break in the lines.

The Columbia Banking sign on Main Street said 8:35 a.m. It also said the temperature had dropped a degree—down to 49 degrees. The rain had turned into a downpour. People ran for cover. The Commerce Building was still standing.

By 9 a.m., people on Main Street had squeezed into doorways to escape the cold rain. On the Broad Street bridge, people had either run for cover or stoically withstood the weather. By now, no one was very cheerful.

That included Haddad. An energetic young man in a sheepskin coat and blue hard hat, Haddad had been running back and forth between the 14th-floor suite and the corner detonation site.

"What's happening? What's happening is a building that was supposed to be down at 7:30 a.m. is still there," he said, looking out the window of the suite.

On the ground, workers were digging nine feet into the ground, searching for the broken connection.

Haddad estimated it would be 10 a.m. before the building was ready to blow, but no one told that to the crowd across the river, standing in the rain. People began to chant and shout.

By 9:15 a.m., the rain stopped. About half the crowd had moved into nearby restaurants and coffee shops, nervously sipping coffee and listening for the sirens. The rumor that it would be 10 a.m. before the blast had somehow begun to circulate, but no announcements had been made.

"Busy—that's not the word for it," said the counter worker at the White Tower on Exchange Street. "It was okay at first, but then we ran out of coffee. We couldn't keep up, and people started getting ugly."

At 9:30 a.m., it was pouring cold rain again. Upstairs, on the 14th floor of the Holiday Inn, people were drinking coffee, whiskey and scotch. Cartoons were playing on a small television over the suite's bar and the rumor now said the warning sirens would sound in 10 minutes.

But there weren't any sirens.

Standing in the rain, the crowd had begun screaming—booing and hissing. People were leaving in a steady stream, running for cars, while a policeman on duty at Four Corners assured angry spectators that the building would be demolished that day. At 10 a.m., half the crowd had disappeared.

In the suite on the 14th floor, word came that the crews were still digging. It would be another 30 to 45 minutes, a crew member estimated. Once the broken wire has been located, it had to be spliced together again and covered, he said.

The rain stopped. A patch of blue even peeked around the Lincoln First Bank building. At 10:45 a.m., police sirens sounded. Wet, cold and tired, the remaining spectators lifted their cameras once again. Everyone was silent.

At 10:55 a.m., police gave the one-minute siren.

"Go, you dirty dog, go," a policeman on the Broad Street bridge yelled. Silence. "It should be gone now. It's all a hoax," he laughed.

Then the building rumbled, tilted slightly and walls collapsed gracefully as dust billowed high into the air, settling around a pile of rubble. From the rumble to the rubble took 11 seconds.

The crowd approved the performance.

"Fantastic!" said Don Bowens, who had been watching the building since 3 a.m. "I wish they'd build it back up and do it again."

A window had been blown out of Mike's Diner, 125 E. Main St, but no injuries were reported.

Discussion Questions

1. What does the headline tell the reader?
2. What is the purpose of the smaller headline?
3. What is the focus of the article—the building or the crowd?
4. What is the purpose of the first sentence?
5. How long did the explosion last?
6. How long did people wait to see it?
7. What was the weather like? Why is this important to the story?
8. How does the writer build interest in the first few sentences?
9. What time did people begin to gather?
10. What time did the explosion occur?
11. What things did people bring with them?
12. What conversations appear in the article? Why does the author include them?
13. What colorful words does the author use to help us see what is being described?
14. What colorful words help us hear what is described?
15. What delayed the detonation?
16. What was the crowd's reaction when the building finally came down?

Describing an Event

We have all attended an interesting event. It may have been a wedding, a graduation, a funeral, a birth, a party, a football game, a birthday party, etc. The exercise below will help you to gather and organize your thoughts so that you can write an essay in which you describe an event of interest to you.

EVENT DESCRIPTION EXERCISE

Planning

Part 1: Think of an event that you remember well and would like to describe. Write the name of the event here.

____

Part 2: Now think of some of the people whom you want to mention. List them here.

____

____

____

Part 3: What parts of the event do you want to describe? Write down your thoughts here.

___

___

___

Part 4: What colorful words (adjectives) can you use so that the reader can see the details?

Details	***Colorful Words***

Part 5: What colorful words can you use so that the reader can hear what is happening? Think about what the event sounded like. You can say it sounded like . . . . .

Details	***Colorful Words***

Part 6: What important information does the reader need to know (background information)? If you are writing about an event in your native country, what information do you need to explain so that someone from another culture can understand it?

Part 7: What special vocabulary words will you use? Do they need to be explained?

____

____

Part 8: How will you begin the essay? (Be sure that the first paragraph introduces what the essay will be about.)

____

____

Part 9: How will you end the essay?

____

____

Part 10: Draw sketches of the various parts of the essay that you wish to describe.

Part 11: Write captions for your sketches in number 10 above.

Writing Your Essay

Part 1: Using all of the information above, tell a classmate about the event. Ask your classmate for suggestions on how you could improve your description of the event. What questions does your classmate ask you? This may be information that you should include in your essay.

Part 2: Write a first draft of your essay.

Part 3: Share the draft with a classmate. Show it to your teacher for input. Make revisions to your draft as needed.

Part 4: Write the essay, using all the information and input you have gathered.

Part 5: When you have finished your essay, share it with your classmates and teacher.

Chapter 6

Writing Dialogues

The goals of this chapter are:

To practice writing at the sentence level within an interesting context

To review sentence information taught in chapter 1

To see how a character's speech effectively portrays the character

To read a radio play

To examine natural speech as a prelude to writing quotations

To learn how to write quotations

To learn the importance of details

Some writing is not presented in paragraph form. It is written as a dialogue, or conversation. Can you think of one type of literature that is written as conversation? If you said a play, you are right. You could also have said a script for a movie, a television program, or even a radio show.

In this chapter, you will read a radio play. Before you read it, glance at it and notice its form. Each person who speaks is named each time he or she speaks. There is a colon (:) after each person's name and then the words that the person is to say. Each time a new person speaks, a new paragraph begins.

As you read this play, there are several things you should be aware of. The first is that all the words spoken are the actual words that the people say. From their words the reader learns a lot about each character. We can hear the character stammer as in "I . . . I . . . I." We can hear a character ramble on and on; we can tell when a character is being abrupt or feeling angry.

As you read, notice the sentences that the author uses. In chapter 1, we studied different types of sentences. Notice how these different sentences are used effectively to express the feelings of the characters and to portray their personalities.

Most of us will not write plays, but we may include quotes in a story to show how a character spoke. We may also use quoted material in a research paper or report.

Your teacher may assign some of you to act the play out in front of the class for fun. What will make it even more exciting is if you choose someone to be responsible for the sound effects—for example, the ringing of the telephone.

Sorry, wrong number

By Lucille Fletcher

CHARACTERS

MRS. STEVENSON
OPERATOR
FIRST MAN
SECOND MAN (*George*)
CHIEF OPERATOR
SERGEANT DUFFY
THIRD MAN (a *Western Union Operator*)
INFORMATION
FOURTH MAN (*a hospital clerk*)

SOUND: *Number being dialed on telephone; then the busy signal.*

MRS. STEVENSON (*a querulous, self-centered neurotic*) (*after waiting a bit*): Oh—*dear!*

SOUND: *Impatient slamming down of receiver; then the sound of dialing again.*

OPERATOR (*filter*): This is the Operator.

MRS. STEVENSON: Operator? I've been dialing 873-0093 now for the last three quarters of an hour, and the line is always busy. But I don't see how it *could* be busy that long. Will you try it for me, please?

OPERATOR (*filter*): I will try it for you. One moment, please.

MRS. STEVENSON (*rambling, full of self-pity*): I don't see how it could be busy all this time. It's my husband's office. He's working late tonight, and I'm all alone here in the house. My health is very poor—and I've been feeling so nervous all day.

OPERATOR (filter): Ringing 873-0093.

SOUND: *Telephone ringing. All clear. It rings three times. The receiver is picked up at the other end.*

MAN'S VOICE (*filter*) (*a slow, heavy, tough voice*): Hello.

MRS. STEVENSON: Hello . . . ? (*A little puzzled*) Hello. Is Mr. Stevenson there?

MAN'S VOICE (*filter*) (*as though he had not heard*): Hello. (*Louder*) Hello!

2ND MAN'S VOICE (*filter*) (*also over telephone but farther away. His voice has a very distinctive quality.*): Hello.

1ST MAN: Hello, George?

GEORGE: Yes, sir.

MRS. STEVENSON (*louder and more imperious*): Hello. Who's this? What number am I calling, please?

1ST MAN: I am in the office with our client. He says the coast is clear for tonight.

GEORGE: Yes, sir.

1ST MAN: Where are you now?

GEORGE: In a phone booth.

1ST MAN: Very well. You know the address. At eleven o'clock the private patrolman goes around to the bar on Second Avenue for a beer. Be sure that all the lights downstairs are out. There should be only one light visible from the street. At eleven-fifteen a subway train crosses the bridge. It makes a noise, in case her window is open and she should scream.

MRS. STEVENSON (*shocked*): Oh! . . . Hello! What number is this, please?

GEORGE: Okay. I understand.

1ST MAN: Make it quick. As little blood as possible. Our client does not wish to make her suffer long.

GEORGE: A knife okay, sir?

1ST MAN: Yes. A knife will be okay. And remember, remove the rings and bracelets—and the jewelry in the bureau drawer. Our client wishes it to look like simple robbery.

SOUND: *The conversation is suddenly cut off. Again there is a persistent buzzing signal.*

MRS. STEVENSON (*clicking phone*): Oh!

SOUND: *Buzzing signal continues. She hangs up slowly.*

MRS. STEVENSON (*frozen with horror*): How awful. How unspeakably—(*A brief pause.*)

SOUND: *She picks up phone and dials Operator. Ring once.*

OPERATOR (*filter*): Your call, please?

MRS. STEVENSON (*unnerved and breathless*): Operator. I—I've just been cut off.

OPERATOR (*filter*): I'm sorry, madam. What number were you calling?

MRS. STEVENSON: Why—it was supposed to be 873-0093—but it wasn't. Some wires must have crossed—I was cut into a wrong number—and I—I've just heard the most dreadful thing—a—a murder—and—(*Imperiously*) Operator, you'll simply have to retrace that call at once.

OPERATOR (*filter*): I'm sorry, madam. I do not understand.

MRS. STEVENSON: Oh—I know it was a wrong number, and I had no business listening, but these two men—they were cold-blooded fiends—and they were going to murder somebody—some poor innocent woman—who was all alone—in a house near a bridge. (*Frantic*) And we've got to stop them—we've got to—

OPERATOR (*filter*) (*patiently*): What number were you calling, madam?

MRS. STEVENSON: That doesn't matter. This was a *wrong* number. And *you* dialed it. And we've got to find out what it was—immediately!

OPERATOR (*filter*): Have you told the police?

MRS. STEVENSON: No, But—in the meantime—

OPERATOR (*filter*): Well, Mrs. Stevenson, I seriously doubt whether we could make this check for you, and trace this call just on your say-so as a private individual. We'd have to have something more official.

MRS. STEVENSON: Oh—for heaven's sake. You mean to tell me—I can't report a murder—without getting tied up in all this red tape? Why, it's perfectly idiotic! All right! I'll call the police!

SOUND: *She slams down receiver.*

MRS. STEVENSON: Ridiculous!

SOUND: *Ring twice.*

SERGEANT DUFFY (*filter*) (*bored with his night duty assignment*): Police Station, Precinct 43, Duffy speaking.

MRS. STEVENSON: Police Department? Oh. This is Mrs. Stevenson—Mrs. Elbert Smythe Stevenson of 53 North Sutton Place. I'm calling up to report a murder. I mean (*Fumbling for words*)—the murder hasn't been committed yet. I just overheard plans for it over the telephone—over a wrong number that the operator gave me. I've been trying to trace down the call myself—but everybody is so stupid—and I guess in the end you're the only people who could *do* anything.

SERGEANT DUFFY (*filter*) (*not too impressed by all this*): Yes, ma'am.

MRS. STEVENSON (*trying to impress him*): It was a perfectly *definite* murder. I heard their plans distinctly. Two men were talking—and they were going to murder some woman at eleven-fifteen tonight. She lived near a bridge.

SERGEANT DUFFY (*filter*): Yes, ma'am.

MRS. STEVENSON: And there was a private patrolman on the street. He was going to go around for a beer on Second Avenue. And there was some third man—a client—who was paying to have this poor woman murdered. They were going to take her rings and bracelets and use a knife. . . . Well—it's unnerved me dreadfully—(*Reaching the breaking point*)—and I'm not well—

SERGEANT DUFFY (*filter*) (*giving her the brush-off*): Well, we'll take care of it, lady. Don't worry.

MRS. STEVENSON: I'd say the whole thing calls for a search—a complete and thorough search of the whole city. I'm very near the bridge—and I'm not far from Second Avenue—and I know *I'd* feel a whole lot better if you sent around a radio car to *this* neighborhood at once!

SERGEANT DUFFY (*filter*): And what makes you think the murder's going to be committed in your neighborhood, ma'am?

MRS. STEVENSON: Oh—I don't know. Only the coincidence is so horrible. Second Avenue—the patrolman—the bridge.

SERGEANT DUFFY (*filter*): Second Avenue is a very long street, ma'am. And do you happen to know how many bridges there are in the city of New York alone? Not to mention Brooklyn, Staten Island, Queens, and the Bronx? Unless, of course, you have some reason for thinking this call is phoney—and that someone may be planning to murder you.

MRS. STEVENSON: Me? Oh—oh, no—I hardly think so. I—I mean why should anybody? I'm alone all day and night. I see nobody except my maid, Eloise. She's a big two-hundred-pounder—she's too lazy to bring up my breakfast tray—and the only other person is my husband, Elbert. He's crazy about me—adores me—waits on me hand and foot—has scarcely left my side since I took sick twelve years ago. . . .

SERGEANT DUFFY (*filter*): Well, then, there's nothing for you to worry about. Now, if you'll just leave the rest to us—

MRS. STEVENSON (*not completely mollified*): But what will you *do*? It's so late. . . . It's nearly eleven now.

SERGEANT DUFFY (*filter*) (*more firmly*): We'll take care of it, lady.

SOUND: *She slams down the receiver hard.*

MRS. STEVENSON: Idiot! (*Pause*) Now, why did I do that? Now he'll think I *am* a fool! (*Pause*) Oh—why doesn't Elbert come home? *Why* doesn't he?

MRS. STEVENSON (*nervously querulous*): If I could only get out of this bed for a little while. If I could get a breath of fresh air—or just lean out the window—and see the street. . . .

SOUND: *The phone rings. She picks it up instantly.*

MRS. STEVENSON: Hello, Elbert? Hello. Hello. Hello. Oh—what's the *matter* with this phone? HELLO. HELLO!

SOUND: *She slams down the receiver. A second's pause. The phone rings again, once. She picks it up.*

MRS. STEVENSON: Hello? Hello . . . Oh, for Heaven's sake, who *is* this? Hello, Hello, HELLO!

SOUND: *She slams down receiver. Then she dials Operator.*

OPERATOR (*filter*): Your call, please?

MRS. STEVENSON (*very annoyed and imperious*): Hello, Operator, I don't know *what's* the matter with this telephone tonight, but it's positively driving me crazy. I've never seen such inefficient, miserable service. Now—I'm an invalid, and I'm very nervous, and I'm *not* supposed to be annoyed. But if this keeps on much longer. . . .

OPERATOR (*filter*): What seems to be the trouble, madam?

MRS. STEVENSON: Well—everything. The whole world could be murdered for all you people care. And now—my phone keeps ringing.

OPERATOR (*filter*): Yes, madam?

MRS. STEVENSON: Ringing and ringing and ringing every five seconds or so—and when I pick it up, there's no one there!

OPERATOR (*filter*): I am sorry, madam. I will test it for you.

MRS. STEVENSON: I don't want you to test it for me. I want you to put that call through—whatever it is—at once!

OPERATOR (*filter*): I am afraid that is not possible, madam. I will try to check it for you madam.

MRS. STEVENSON: Check it. Check it. That's all anybody can do. Oh—I'm going out of my mind with all you people!

SOUND: *She slams down the receiver. Almost instantly the phone rings. She picks up the receiver.*

MRS. STEVENSON (*her nerves getting scratchier and scratchier*): Hello. HELLO! Stop ringing, do you hear? Answer me. Who *is* this? Do you realize you're driving me crazy? Who's calling me? What are you doing it for? Now stop it—Stop it, I say. HELLO. HELLO! If you don't stop ringing me, I'm going to call the police—do you hear? The POLICE!

SOUND: *She slams down the receiver.*

MRS. STEVENSON (*sobbing nervously*): If Elbert would only come home!

SOUND: *The phone rings again sharply.*

MRS. STEVENSON: Let it ring. Let it go on ringing. It's a trick of some kind. And I won't answer it. I won't—even if it goes on ringing all night. . . . Oh—stop it—stop it. I can't stand any more.

SOUND: *She picks up receiver.*

MRS. STEVENSON (*yelling frenziedly into phone*): Hello. What do you want? Stop ringing, will you? Stop it—oh. (*In a subdued voice*) I'm sorry. Yes. This is 754-2293.

3RD MAN (*filter*): This is Western Union. I have a telegram here for Mrs. Elbert Stevenson. Is there anyone there to receive the message?

MRS. STEVENSON (*trying to calm herself*): I am Mrs. Stevenson.

3RD MAN (*filter*): The telegram is as follows: Mrs. Elbert Stevenson, 53 North Sutton Place, New York, New York. Darling. Terribly sorry. Tried to get you for last hour, but line busy. Leaving for Boston eleven P.M. tonight, on urgent business. Back tomorrow afternoon. Keep happy. Love. Signed, Elbert.

MRS. STEVENSON (*breathlessly, almost to herself*): Oh—no—

3RD MAN (*filter*): That is all, madam. Do you wish us to deliver a copy of the message?

MRS. STEVENSON: No. No, thank you.

3RD MAN (*filter*): Very well, madam. Good night.

SOUND: *He hangs up.*

MRS. STEVENSON (*mechanically*): Good night.

SOUND: *She hangs up.*

MRS. STEVENSON (*suddenly bursting out*): No. No—I don't believe it. He couldn't do it. Not when he knows I'll be all alone. It's some trick—some fiendish—

SOUND: *Mrs. Stevenson nervously dials the number. It comes through, ring after long ring. No answer.*

MRS. STEVENSON: He's gone. Oh—Elbert—how could you—

SOUND: *She hangs up the phone.*

MRS. STEVENSON (*sobs, pitying herself*): But I can't be alone—tonight. I can't. If I'm alone one more second, I'll go mad. I don't care what he says—or what the expense is—I'm sick—I'm entitled—

SOUND: *She dials Information.*

INFORMATION (*filter*): This is Information.

MRS. STEVENSON: I want the telephone number of Henchley Hospital.

INFORMATION (*filter*): Henchley Hospital? Do you have the address, madam?

MRS. STEVENSON: No. It's somewhere in the seventies. It's a very small, private, and exclusive hospital where I had my appendix out two years ago. Henchley. H-e-n-c—

INFORMATION (*filter*): One moment, please.

MRS. STEVENSON: Please hurry. And please—what *is* the time?

INFORMATION (*filter*): I do not know, madam. You may find out the time by dialing 337-1212.

MRS. STEVENSON (*irritated*): Oh, for heaven's sake—

INFORMATION (*filter*): The number of Henchley Hospital is 287-0105, madam.

MRS. STEVENSON: 287-0105.

SOUND: *She hangs up before she finishes speaking, and starts to dial the number even as she speaks. It rings.*

4TH MAN (*filter*) (*middle-aged, solid, firm, practical*): Henchley Hospital. Good evening.

MRS. STEVENSON: Nurses' Registry.

4TH MAN (*filter*): Who was it you wished to speak to, please?

MRS. STEVENSON (*high-handed*): I want the Nurse's Registry, at once. I want a trained nurse. I want to hire her immediately. For the night.

4TH MAN (*filter*): I see. And what is the nature of the case, madam?

MRS. STEVENSON: Nerves. I'm very nervous. I need soothing—and companionship. You see—my husband is away—and I'm—

4TH MAN (*filter*) (*calmly*): I see. Well, I'll speak to Miss Phillips as soon as she comes in. And what is your name, madam?

MRS. STEVENSON: Miss Phillips? And what time do you expect her in?

4TH MAN (*filter*): I really don't know, madam. She went out to supper at eleven o'clock.

MRS. STEVENSON: Eleven o'clock! But it's not eleven yet! (*She cries out.*) Oh—my clock *has* stopped. I *thought* it was running down. What time is it?

4TH MAN (*filter*) (*pausing as though glancing at wrist watch*): Just fifteen minutes past eleven.

SOUND: *Telephone receiver being lifted on the same line as Mrs. Stevenson's.*

MRS. STEVENSON (*crying out*): What was *that*?

4TH MAN (*filter*): What was what, madam?

MRS. STEVENSON: That—that click—just now—in my own telephone. As though someone had lifted the receiver off the hook of the extension telephone downstairs.

4TH MAN (*filter*): I didn't hear it, madam. Now—about this—

MRS. STEVENSON (*terrified*): But—I *did*. There's someone in this house. Someone downstairs—in the kitchen. And they're listening to me now. They're—(She *screams*.)

SOUND: *She hangs up. Then silence.*

MRS. STEVENSON (*in a suffocated voice*): I won't pick it up. I won't let them hear me. I'll be quiet—and they'll think— (*With growing terror*) but if I don't call someone now—while they're still down there—there'll be no time. . . .

SOUND: *She picks up the receiver and dials Operator. Ring three times.*

OPERATOR (*filter*): Your call, please?

MRS. STEVENSON (*in a desperate whisper*): Operator. I—I'm in desperate trouble. I—

OPERATOR (*filter*): I cannot hear you, madam. Please speak louder.

MRS. STEVENSON (*still whispering*): I don't dare. I—there's someone listening. Can you hear me now?

OPERATOR (*filter*): No, madam.

MRS. STEVENSON (*desperately*): But you've got to hear me. Oh—please. You've got to help me. There's someone in this house. Someone who's going to murder me. And you've got to get in touch with the—

SOUND: *Click of receiver being put down in Mrs. Stevenson's line.*

MRS. STEVENSON (*bursting out wildly*): Oh—there it is. He's put it down—he's put down the extension phone. He's—coming up. (*Her voice is hoarse with fear.*) He's coming up the stairs. Give me the Police Department—the—

OPERATOR (*filter*): One moment, please.

SOUND: *Call is put through. Phone rings at other end. On second ring Mrs. Stevenson starts to scream. She screams twice as the phone continues to ring. On the fourth scream the sound of a subway train is heard as it roars over a nearby bridge. It drowns out all sound for a second. Then it passes and the phone can be heard still ringing at the other end. The telephone is picked up.*

SERGEANT DUFFY (*filter*): Police Station, Precinct 43, Duffy speaking. (*A pause, then louder*) Police Department. Sergeant Duffy speaking.

GEORGE (*same distinctive voice as in beginning of play*): Sorry. Wrong number.

SOUND: *He hangs up.*

ABOUT THE AUTHOR • Lucille Fletcher (1912–   ) grew up in Brooklyn, New York, not far from the Queensboro Bridge, important in "Sorry, Wrong Number." After college she worked as a jack-of-all-trades for the Columbia Broadcasting System. Although she had been writing stories almost all her life, she had never attempted a radio script. But when one of her stories was adapted for radio, she decided to try her hand. Miss Fletcher has been doing radio and television scripts ever since.

"Sorry, Wrong Number" continues to be her biggest success. How did she happen to write such a thriller? "I wrote 'Sorry, Wrong Number' because I wanted to write something that could be performed only on the air," Miss Fletcher says. "It took me about two months to think out this piece and about three days to write it. The character of Mrs. Stevenson is based on an actual person I once ran into in a grocery. The only thing not authentic is the train on the Queensboro Bridge. Subway trains no longer run across it."

Discussion Questions

1. Who is Mrs. Stevenson?

2. What do we know about her at the beginning of the play?

3. Who does she call? Does she reach him? Why not?

4. What kind of information appears in parentheses in a play?

5. What is special about Mrs. Stevenson? Why does she stay in bed?

6. What does she overhear?

7. Why does she become upset?

8. What does she do to try to prevent a murder?

9. Does she know who is going to be murdered?

10. Does she know who the murderer is?

11. What happens when she calls the police department?

12. What happens when she tells the operator what she knows?

13. Who is the murderer?

14. When did you realize that she was to be the victim?

15. There is no action in this play, yet the writer creates a lot of suspense. How does she do that?

WRITING DIALOGUES EXERCISE 1

Part A

Think of an important conversation that you have had with someone. It could be a conversation with a friend, a parent, a sister, a brother, a teacher, an uncle, etc. Why do you remember this conversation? What was special about it?

First, write a one- or two-sentence introduction to tell the reader some background information. For example, tell the reader who this person is and where the conversation took place. You might also discuss why you had this conversation.

Now write down the conversation. Each time a new person speaks, use the name of the person followed by a colon. Then write exactly what the person said. In a dialogue you cannot say "He said." You must just say the person's actual words.

Think about some of the information the reader can't see. For example, what does the person look like? How is he or she dressed? Where does the conversation take place? What does the room look like? Are there any sounds in the background? A train, a television, a baby crying, birds singing, a waterfall, a tea kettle? Think about these things, and then include only those things that are important. Put this information in parentheses.

Write your dialogue on a separate sheet of paper.

Part B

Exchange dialogues with a classmate. Read the dialogue and write down any questions you have. Then use the questions below as a guide.

1. Has the author told you everything you need to know?

---

2. Does the conversation sound real?

---

3. What is the purpose of the conversation? Was the purpose clear to you? Does the author agree with you that that was his or her purpose?

---

4. Is there enough descriptive information so that you know what the people look like or how old they are? What details did you like?

____

5. Do you feel like you know the people and their personalities as a result of reading the dialogue?

____

6. Do you know what the setting is?

____

7. Did you have enough background information to understand the dialogue and the people? What could the author have added to help you? What did the author tell you that was helpful?

____

____

8. Are the spelling, grammar, and sentence structure good? What suggestions do you have?

____

9. Are the words colorful? What vocabulary words might you suggest?

____

Meet with the author and share this information. Then rewrite your dialogue.

WRITING DIALOGUES EXERCISE 2

Think of a famous person either living or dead whom you wish you could have a conversation with. Using the guide questions below, write a dialogue between you and this person.

Guide Questions

1. Write the name of this person.

____

2. Explain who he or she is.

____

3. Explain why you would like to meet this person.

___

4. Describe what this person looks like.

___

5. Write a list of questions you would like to ask this person.

a. ___

b. ___

c. ___

d. ___

e. ___

f. ___

6. How do you think this person would answer each of these questions? Write your ideas below.

a. ___

b. ___

c. ___

d. ___

e. ___

f. ___

7. Aside from your questions, what would you like to tell this person?

___

8. What do you think this person will say to what you tell him or her?

___

9. What do you think this person may want to tell *you*?

___

After you have answered these questions, write a dialogue with this person. Use a separate sheet of paper. Be prepared to share your dialogue with a classmate or the class.

WRITING QUOTATIONS EXERCISE 1

Read the headline in the article below. What does it mean? What is Carhenge? Have you ever heard of Stonehenge? What is it? Where is it? If you don't know, look it up in an encyclopedia.

Read the article and answer the questions that follow.

'Carhenge' in Nebraska: monument or junkyard?

By Paul Simon

The Associated Press

ALLIANCE, Neb.—From a distance, it is a stark, desolate array of odd gray columns. Up close, it is an eerie display of automobile history.

Art or junk, this creation of old vehicles called Carhenge attracts hundreds of people to the sand hills of northwestern Nebraska, where residents are debating whether the monument—or automobile graveyard—should be preserved.

James Reinders, a Houston oil consultant, created Carhenge in 1987 as a takeoff on the ancient religious and astronomical site Stonehenge on Salisbury Plain in England. Instead of colossal stones, he used cars.

He arranged 22 aging Plymouths, Fords, Chevrolets—even an ambulance—in a wheat field two miles north of Alliance. Sixteen cars are planted trunk down with their front ends in the air. Six more sit atop them, forming arches.

In Alliance, a community of 9,900, city officials are debating whether to enforce a permit that requires Reinders to pave the entry to Carhenge by July 15, 1990, or see it torn down.

A group called Friends of Carhenge, headed by City Councilman Paul Phaneuf, incorporated and wants to raise the $2,000 for the paving.

Reinders says he pays for liability on his property and is not interested in paying for paving.

"This is really good for Alliance and it didn't cost anybody anything," said Phaneuf. "Finally, someone has given us something of value."

"It's wonderful for us," said Martin Marnett, manager of a local fast-food restaurant. "It has created so much interest . . . and it does put a grin on your face."

On Thursday, the council will vote on a request to change the zoning of the land from agricultural to commercial, eliminating the need for paving.

Janet Steele, executive director of the Alliance Chamber of Commerce, said Carhenge detractors were vocal until a comment box was installed at the site in August. It drew 425 responses in the first 20 days, most of them overwhelmingly favorable.

Critics argue the car pile should be torn down because it is unsightly. Some say it is nothing more than a junkyard.

Besides Carhenge and the annual Heritage Days in July, there isn't much to bring people to Alliance. Highway 2 runs east through town into the scenic sand hills, but for out-of-state folks, the closest wonder is Mount Rushmore three hours away in South Dakota.

Sculpture made up of junked cars is based on historic Stonehenge. (Reprinted with permission of the *Times-Union* and *Democrat and Chronicle*, Rochester, NY (October 29, 1988), 6C.)

Discussion Questions

1. What is Carhenge?

___

2. Where is it?

___

3. Why has it been given this name?

___

4. Who is James Reinders?

___

5. How many cars did he use?

___

6. What kind of cars are they?

___

7. What is the problem? What are the city officials debating?

___

8. What do the local citizens think about Carhenge?

---

9. How many favorable responses did they get in a comment box? What is a comment box?

---

10. Why is Carhenge important to Alliance?

---

11. Would you like to go to see Carhenge? Why or why not?

---

12. Look at the quoted material in paragraphs 8 and 9. The material begins and ends with quotation marks (" "). What is the reason for these marks of punctuation? What do they tell the reader?

---

13. How are quotes written? Where do the quotation marks go?

---

14. Where do the commas go in a quotation?

---

15. Where does the period go?

---

16. Who are the people quoted?

---

17. What do the quotes add to the story?

---

18. What would the story be like without the quoted material?

---

19. When is quoted material used?

---

20. When you read the newspaper, who is usually quoted?

____

21. In a quote, can the writer change any of the words that the speaker said?

____

22. Ask a classmate what he or she thinks about Carhenge. Write your classmate's exact words here.

____

23. Now introduce what your friend said by writing your friend's name and the word "said." Put a comma after "said." Use quotation marks before and after your friends' words. Write your friend's exact words here.

____

You have now written a quotation in English!

WRITING QUOTATIONS EXERCISE 2

There are many famous quotations:

Hamlet said, "To be or not to be? That is the question."

President Franklin Delano Roosevelt comforted the American public during World War II when he said, "The only thing we have to fear is fear itself."

President John F. Kennedy told Americans, "Ask not what your country can do for you—ask what you can do for your country."

What famous quotations do you know? Write some of them here.

____

____

____

WRITING QUOTATIONS EXERCISE 3

Quotes are used as support for a writer's idea. Famous people are quoted in the press every day. Scientists, actors, scholars, clergypeople, historians, and politicians are quoted in journals, magazines, and newspapers. Look in magazines and newspapers and cut out some articles in which people are quoted. Paste or tape them on the space on the next page.

WRITING QUOTATIONS EXERCISE 4

There are certain rules that must be followed when quoting someone.

1. The most important rule is that you cannot change the words the person uses. You are quoting someone; therefore, you must use their exact words. Even if the person makes a mistake by presenting wrong information or using poor grammar, the person writing the quote may not change it.
2. When you use the person's exact words, you must put quotation marks before and after the exact words. The quotation marks that precede the words tell the reader that the next words are exactly what the person said. The quotation marks that come after the quoted material tell the reader that this is the end of the quote.
3. Quotes are often introduced by introductory words such as *he said, she asked, he replied, they responded,* etc. When you use introductory words, place a comma after the introductory words.
   For example:

   She said, "Don't forget to call."
   He replied, "I won't."

4. You can also write the quoted material first and then write *he said* or *she said.* Then you must put the comma before the last quotation mark. For example:

   "Don't forget to call," she said.
   "I won't," he replied.

5. Punctuation marks are important when you write quotes. Look at the examples above. In the examples under number 3, where do the commas go? In the examples under number 4, where do the commas go?
6. Where does the period go in the examples under number 3 above? Is the comma before or after the quotation marks?
7. Where does the comma go in the examples under number 4? Does the comma go before or after the quotation marks?
8. Look at the quotes you cut out of magazines and newspapers. Note where the punctuation is in these quotes.

WRITING QUOTATIONS EXERCISE 5

To practice using the information you have just learned on how to use quotation marks, add the missing quotation marks and the correct punctuation to the conversation below.

Susan asked me yesterday, Do you like your English class?
I said yes.
She said But you didn't like it before.
I said I know, but this year we are doing more interesting things.
Oh she said. What are you doing?
We are writing dialogues I replied.
What is a dialogue she asked.
I said it's a conversation between two people just like we are having now.

WRITING QUOTATIONS EXERCISE 6

In this exercise, you will learn how to incorporate quoted material into your writing.

1. Read the article on page 125, which has one quote in it.
2. Ask a classmate for his or her opinion about the situation.
3. Write down your classmate's exact words.
4. Decide where you would have put your classmate's quote if you had been the author of this article.
5. Draw a line from the exact spot in the article where you want to put the quote to a wide space in the margin.
6. Then write your classmate's name and what he or she said. Use the correct form for quoting material.

Adults stifle girls' interest in science: Teen-age girls also taught to shun math

Cox News Service

Little girls love math and science almost as much as little boys do, but by the time girls reach high school, teachers and family members have convinced most of them that they'd best avoid technical subjects, a survey shows.

Despite widespread belief that teens' attitudes are shaped largely by other teens, researchers with the American Association of University Women found that school officials and family members in fact do far more to make girls feel incompetent and to steer them away from science careers.

They based their findings on a survey of 3,000 U.S. youngsters. A summary report, called *Shortchanging Girls, Shortchanging America,* was released Wednesday in Washington.

The survey found a link between the loss of interest in math and science and a phenomenon that has been noticed for years: little girls like themselves but adolescent girls are riddled with self-doubt.

Sixty percent of the girls questioned felt good about themselves in elementary school, but that percentage dropped to 37 by middle school and to 29 by high school. Boys' self-esteem fell from 67 to 56 percent in middle school, and to 46 percent in high school.

"The research, particularly the focus groups, shows that young women find people, including their teachers, believing that females cannot do the things they believe they can," the survey report said. "The result is girls' lower self-esteem."

WRITING QUOTATIONS EXERCISE 7

Read the article about a "Future Hotel" on page 126. Underline parts of the article you might want to quote if you were to write an article on the subject. Then write a short article with two quotes taken from this article. In your article, discuss the effect modern technology has on our lives.

Notice that when we wrote the title of this article we put it in quotation marks. Another use of quotation marks is to put them around titles of articles, titles of chapters in books, names of movies, and names of television shows.

Future hotel: check in and out by pressing some buttons

By Jerry Flemmons

Fort Worth Star-Telegram

OK, it's the year 2001 and you're checking into a hotel. All you do is walk to the front desk, slip your credit card into a slot and out drops an electronic key card.

You take the card, which has printed instructions on how to find your room. You open your room door and find a fax machine, a personal computer and other electronic gadgetry, including a VCR and a supply of current movies to watch later in the evening. The fridge is filled with light snacks. There will be complimentary wine and fruit.

A couple of days later, you check out by punching buttons on the television set, which shows you an itemized bill that will be charged to your credit card. Grab your bags and you're gone.

That's what hoteliers are predicting for the traveler still out there on the road in the early 21st century.

Said one report on the future of hotel management: "No lines, no frustrating waits to make you late for a plane or meeting."

And no humans to help. The future may not be very much fun.

Reprinted with permission of the *Times-Union* and *Democrat and Chronicle*, Rochester, NY (September 23, 1990), 7C.

WRITING QUOTATIONS EXERCISE 8

There are many issues today on which people have different views. Some people believe that children should wear uniforms to school, others are opposed to this; some people believe that the speed limit on highways should be sixty-five miles per hour, while others prefer a fifty-five mile per hour limit. Think of several controversial issues that people are discussing today. They may have to do with your school, your city or town, politics, world events, or social issues. List some of these issues in the space below.

____

____

____

Your teacher may ask you to put your topics on the board. When all the topics are on the board, choose one that is of particular interest to you. (Each student should choose a different topic.) Write the one you choose on the line below.

My controversial issue: ________________________________

In the space below write several questions related to the topic. One of them should ask your classmates for their opinion on the controversial issue you have chosen.

My Questions for the Interview

1. ______________________________

2. ______________________________

3. ______________________________

4. ______________________________

Interview five classmates by asking them these questions. Be sure to ask each person the same questions.

Write your classmate's name and his or her exact words in response to each question in the chart below.

Person interviewed	*Their exact words in response to each question*
Name #1 ____________	1. ____________ ____________ ____________ 2. ____________ ____________ ____________ 3. ____________ ____________ ____________ 4. ____________ ____________ ____________

Name #2 ______________________

1. ______________________

____

____

2. ______________________

____

____

3. ______________________

____

____

4. ______________________

____

____

Name #3 ______________________

1. ______________________

____

____

2. ______________________

____

____

3. ______________________

____

____

4. ______________________

____

____

Name #4 ______________________

1. ______________________

____

____

2. ______________________

____

____

3. ______________________

____

____

4. ______________________

____

____

Name #5 ______________________

1. ______________________

____

____

2. ______________________

____

____

3. ______________________

____

____

4. ______________________

____

____

WRITING QUOTATIONS EXERCISE 9

In preparation for writing an article about how your classmates feel about your controversial issue, here are some guide questions. These questions indicate the information you should include in your essay.

1. What is the controversial issue you have chosen?
2. What is your opinion on this issue?
3. What questions did you ask in your survey?
4. How many people did you ask?
5. How many people had the same opinion on each question? Fill in the chart below.

	Same opinion	*Different opinion*
question 1	______________	______________
question 2	______________	______________
question 3	______________	______________
question 4	______________	______________

6. How many people had the same opinion that you had? How many had a different opinion than you?

____

7. What reasons did people give for their opinions?

____

8. What quotes would you want to include in your article?

____

9. What does your survey show about how people feel on this issue?

____

Using the information you have gathered from your survey, write on a separate sheet of paper a short article in which you report your results. Be sure to state what the issue is, how you went about getting people's opinions, and what the opinions indicated. Include one or two quotes in your article. As you write the conclusion, think about what the survey showed and what these results may mean.

Chapter 7

Telling Stories and Writing Parodies

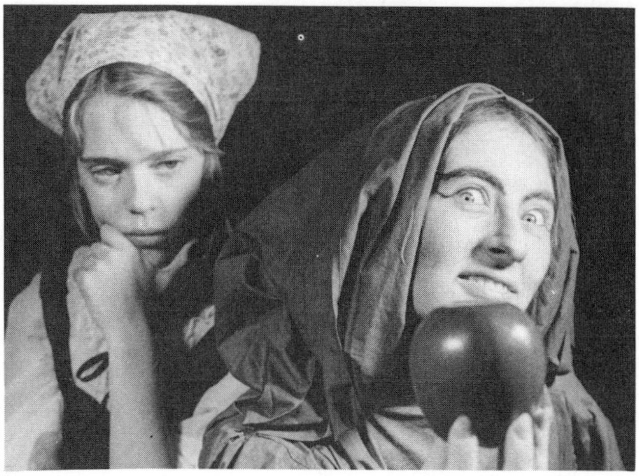

The goals for this chapter are:

To focus on the parts of a story

- characters
- plot
- setting

To apply information previously learned

- summarizing
- using descriptive words
- writing dialogue
- using quotes

To use guided writing

To use guided editing

In chapter 3, you learned to capture the main idea and to summarize. In the previous chapter, you learned how to write dialogue. In this chapter, you will combine both of these skills to write a summary of a children's story. It may be a fairy tale, a fable or folk tale, or other type of children's story. You will also learn what parody is, and you will have a chance to write a parody.

Before you tell your story, let's look at a fairy tale that is popular in many parts of the world. As you read it, you may find that it sounds similar to a story that you know. Sometimes when stories are told in different countries, parts of the story change; often the endings are different.

The story below is called "Little Red Riding Hood."

Once upon a time, a little girl's mother asked her to take a basket of food to her sick grandmother. The little girl put on her red jacket with a red hood. Her mother gave her a basket of food and cautioned her, "Be careful in the woods. Don't talk to anyone, and stay on the path."

Little Red Riding Hood left the house. As she walked through the woods, she saw some pretty flowers and stepped off the path to pick some for her grandmother. Suddenly a wolf appeared from behind a tree, and he asked her where she was going. She said, "I am going to my grandmother's house, but I can't talk to anyone."

"Where does your grandmother live?" he asked.

Little Red Riding Hood told him. The wolf said goodbye, and he left. Little Red Riding Hood continued on her way.

In a little while, she arrived at her grandmother's house. She went into the bedroom. When she saw her grandmother, she said, "Grandma, what big eyes you have!"

"The better to see you with, my dear," said Grandma.

"But Grandma, what big ears you have!"

"The better to hear you with, my dear," said Grandma.

"But Grandma, what big teeth you have!" exclaimed Little Red Riding Hood.

"The better to eat you with, my dear!" the wolf said, as he sprang from the bed. Little Red Riding Hood screamed, and a nearby woodcutter heard her cries. He came running to the house and shot and killed the wolf.

Moral of the story: Don't talk to strangers. Listen to your mother.

There are many versions of "Little Red Riding Hood." Have you heard the story before? Do you remember the story the same way? What was different in the story that you heard as a child?

What is a moral? Why do children's stories often have morals?

If you were Little Red Riding Hood, what would you have written in your diary that night?

Telling Stories

Now you will have an opportunity to retell a fairy tale that you remember. The exercise below will guide you as you remember your story and plan how to tell it.

STORYTELLING EXERCISE

Planning

Part 1: Answer these questions as you begin to plan your story.

1. Think of a simple story. Choose one that is short and that will be easy to tell in English. Write the title here.

____

2. Where does the story take place? Does it take place in a city, town, or village? Does it take place in a particular country? Is this important for the reader to know?

____

3. Who are the characters?

____

____

____

4. What happens in the story?

____

____

____

5. How does the story begin?

6. How does the story end?

7. Do the characters talk to each other? What do they say? Write some of their conversations here. Be sure to use quotation marks where necessary.

8. Are there any special vocabulary words that the reader will need to know? Write them here. If they need to be explained, then explain them here too.

Part 2: Sketch with simple drawings the scenes in the story.

Part 3: Number the sketches to make sure that they are in the right order.

Part 4: Write captions for each picture.

Writing Your Story

Part 1: Using the sketches, tell the story to a classmate. Ask for suggestions to help improve your telling of the story.

Part 2: Write a draft of your story. If you learned this story in another language, it is important not to translate. Tell the story in English without thinking about the words in another language.

Part 3: Exchange stories with a classmate. It should be a different classmate from the one you told the story to before.

Part 4: Student editors should respond on a separate sheet of paper to the following questions:

1. Does the story make sense?
2. Do you understand everything? If not, what don't you understand?
3. Are the events in the story in the proper order? What would you change?
4. Has any information been omitted that would help you understand the story better?
5. Does the beginning tell the reader what the story will be about?
6. Does the story have an ending? Is it an effective ending?
7. Does the story have dialogue? Does the dialogue help you to know the characters better?
8. Are the words spelled correctly?

9. Is the grammar correct?
10. Is the sentence structure good? What sentences might you change?
11. Does the author use colorful words? Which ones do you especially like?
12. What colorful words do you suggest the author include?

Editing Your Story

Part 1: Take your editor's suggestions into consideration and make changes in your story. As you edit the story, think of other ways you can improve it.

Part 2: Think about ways to improve your choice of words. Have you used words that are precise? Do they help the reader to see and hear the characters? Are the verbs the best action words you could think of?

In chapter 2, we studied parts of speech and talked about the importance of different types of words. Notice how substituting different verbs for the general words in the chart below changes the meaning and gives the reader a better picture of the person or action. Check your dictionary for any meanings you don't understand. Then act out for the class how you would walk if you sauntered, limped, rushed, strolled, and so forth. Why is using precise words important?

General word	***Better descriptor***
walked	sauntered, limped, rushed, strolled, hurried
little	short, young, small, tiny, miniscule, microscopic
child	youngster, son, daughter, toddler, infant, kid, baby, teenager, adolescent

Watch how this story can be changed by altering a few words.

Sam	rushed	into the classroom late. It was the	third	time this
	limped		*first*	
	sauntered		*100th*	
	strolled			
	walked		_____	
	hurried			
	_____			

week.	Everyone	looked up at him. He	smiled	and	quickly	took
year.	*No one*		*frowned*		*slowly*	
month.	*Mary*		*laughed*		*noisily*	
	Mr. Collins				*quietly*	
_____			_____			
	_____				_____	
his seat.						

The feeling that the reader gets for a character or a story depends a great deal on the words the author chooses to use. In the short description above, what do you know about Sam if you read the story using the first set of words?

What do you think about Sam if you read the story using the third set of words? What gives you a different opinion of him?

Part 3: Rewrite your story, taking all of the above information and questions into consideration.

Writing Parodies

What is a parody? A parody is a humorous or exaggerated representation of something familiar. In a parody, a writer takes a familiar story and changes it by exaggerating some of the things that happen or by making it funny.

WRITING PARODIES EXERCISE 1

James Thurber, a famous American humorist and cartoonist, wrote a parody of "Little Red Riding Hood." Read his version of the children's story below.

The little girl and the wolf

One afternoon a big wolf waited in a dark forest for a little girl to come along carrying a basket of food to her grandmother. Finally a little girl did come along and she was carrying a basket of food. "Are you carrying that basket to your grandmother?" asked the wolf. The little girl said yes, she was. So the wolf asked her where her grandmother lived and the little girl told him and he disappeared into the wood.

When the little girl opened the door of her grandmother's house she saw that there was somebody in bed with a nightcap and nightgown on. She had approached no nearer than twenty-five feet from the bed when she saw that it was not her grandmother but the wolf, for even in a nightcap a wolf does not look any more like your grandmother than the Metro-Goldwyn lion looks like Calvin Coolidge. So the little girl took an automatic out of her basket and shot the wolf dead.

Moral: It is not so easy to fool little girls nowadays as it used to be.

Discussion Questions

1. Who are the characters in this story? How are they different from those in the first version of the story?
2. What is the girl doing when she meets the wolf?
3. What does the wolf ask her?
4. Does she answer him?
5. What does the little girl see when she gets to her grandmother's house?
6. What is the Metro-Goldwyn lion? Who was Calvin Coolidge? Why does Thurber mention them?
7. What does the little girl do when she recognizes the wolf?
8. What is the moral of the story?
9. How is this story the same as "Little Red Riding Hood?" How is it different? Fill in the chart below.

Similarities	*Differences*

As we mentioned before, we use the word *parody* to describe a story that is based on another story but that makes fun of it. Thurber's parody modernizes "Little Red Riding Hood." The moral of the story is more appropriate to today's society.

If you were James Thurber's "Little Red Riding Hood," what would you write in your journal or diary tonight?

WRITING PARODIES EXERCISE 2

Go back to your story. Read it and think about how you could change it into a parody.

What words can you change? What aspect of life today would you like to make fun of or make a statement about?

Planning

Part 1: What point would you like to make about today's society? How can you use your story to do that?

Part 2: Consider each of the parts of your story. Do not change all of them. If you do, you will have a completely different story.

Use the chart below to guide you in thinking about the parts of your story.

Component	*Old story*	*New story*
setting (place)	____________	____________
characters	____________	____________
plot (story)	____________	____________
dialogue	____________	____________
moral	____________	____________
vocabulary	____________	____________

Part 3: Notice how Thurber's story summarizes the old story rather than retelling it. Keeping this in mind, answer these questions:

1. How will you begin your story?

____

2. How will you end your story?

____

Part 4: Draw rough sketches of the segments of your new story in this space and on the next page. Use as many sketches as you need. You do not have to use all of them in the final story.

Part 5: Write captions for the sketches you have drawn. Try to update as many things as you can. Use modern-day dress, scenery, and language wherever possible.

Writing Your Parody

Part 1: Using the sketches, tell the story to a classmate. Ask your classmate for suggestions or ideas to improve your story.

Part 2: Write a draft of your story.

Part 3: Exchange papers with another student in your class. (Give your classmate both the fairy tale and the parody.) Read them and write your comments on a separate sheet of paper. Use the following questions as a guide.

1. Is the story clear and easy to understand?
2. Is it a parody?
3. Does it have a moral?
4. What is the moral of the story?
5. Is the vocabulary colorful? Does it help you to see and hear the story more clearly? What words would you suggest the author use to improve the descriptions in the story?
6. Do you have other suggestions?
7. How does the story compare with the person's original story? Which one do you like better? Why?
8. Does the dialogue sound real? How might you change it? What do you especially like? Is there one line that someone says that you especially appreciate? If so, what is it?

9. Is there one character you like best? Why?

10. Now focus on the mechanics of the writing.

    Is the spelling correct?
    Is the grammar correct?
    Are the sentences clear?
    Have quotes been used correctly?

11. What suggestions for revision do you have?

Part 4: Return the story and your comments to the author. Discuss your reactions to the stories you have read.

Editing Your Parody

Rewrite and edit your parody, using all the information and input you have gathered.

Chapter 8

Writing Reviews

The goals for this chapter are:

To analyze reviews

To use summarizing techniques

To include important details

To appreciate different points of view

To use peer review and guided writing

To express an opinion and support it with evidence

A review is a comment on how good or bad something is. Reviews are used to tell the public about movies, books, restaurants, plays, symphonies, operas, records, and other forms of entertainment. A review helps people decide whether to read the book, see the movie, or go to the play. In a review, the reviewer usually gives the reader a brief summary or overview of what is being reviewed and then comments on the quality of the performance.

The things that a reviewer would say in a review are not much different from the things you might tell a friend about an experience you had at a restaurant or your response to a new movie.

In fact, before we go to a new restaurant, we often ask a friend if he or she has eaten there. We ask about the food, the service, the cost, and the atmosphere. Before we go to a movie, we may want to know what kind of movie it is, who is starring in it, and how good the story is.

In each case, we have asked our friend to give us a review. In this chapter, we will read reviews of movies and restaurants, and you will have an opportunity to write a review of your own.

Analyzing Movie Advertisements

Ads are an important means of attracting people to a movie. Before you begin writing movie reviews, look at some advertisements ("ads") for movies in a newspaper and bring them to class. Read the ad on page 145 as well as the ads you brought in and be prepared to answer the following questions:

1. What kinds of information do advertisers include in movie ads? Does it make you want to see the movie? Why or why not?

____

2. What types of words do advertisers use in movie ads? List some of them below. How effective are these words?

____

3. What is the purpose of the quoted material? Is it effective?

____

4. What kinds of information appear in most ads?

____

5. Would these ads interest you in seeing the movie? Why or why not?

____

Reprinted, by permission, from the Walt Disney Company.

Analyzing Movie Reviews

Below are movie reviews that appeared in the newspaper. Please read them. If you saw any of these movies, be ready to indicate whether you agree or disagree with the reviewer. As you read the reviews, think about the type of information that the reviewer includes.

Movie capsules

Capsulized reviews by **Jack Garner,** *Democrat and Chronicle* film critic, provide a guide to movies playing at area theaters. Ratings guide: ★★★★ Excellent ★★★ Good ★★ Fair ★ Poor.

Almost an Angel (PG)—*"Crocodile" Dundee* star Paul Hogan falls on his face in this inept change-of-pace film. He stars as a thief who believes he's become an angel and must do good deeds to earn permanent status. His efforts help a community center and a young man in a wheelchair, and fill the screen with oft-repeated jokes, predictability, skimpy special effects and hollow sentimentality. Frank Capra, he ain't. 96 mins. ★

Avalon (PG)—Barry Levinson's talent for exploring universal themes in his personal background reaches full maturity in the most moving film yet from the director of *Diner, Tin Men, The Natural* and *Rain Man.* The latest of the director's so-called "Baltimore movies." *Avalon* details the story of three generations of a Jewish immigrant family. The ensemble cast is headed by Armin Mueller-Stahl, Joan Plowright, Aidan Quinn and Elizabeth Perkins. 126 mins. ★★★★

The Bonfire of the Vanities (R)—Brian DePalma's eagerly awaited film is an occasionally fascinating, more often frustrating re-interpretation of Tom Wolfe's powerhouse novel about racism, class struggle and modern life in New York. Never boring but amazingly wrong-headed, this movie is the darnedest, most entertaining failure of the holiday season. Tom Hanks stars as Sherman McCoy, a would-be "master of the universe," a wealthy WASP Manhattan stockbroker whose upscale Fifth Avenue life crumbles one night when he and his mistress (Melanie Griffith) take a wrong turn in the Bronx. Morgan Freeman and a most inappropriate Bruce Willis co-star. 125 mins. ★★

Cyrano de Bergerac (PG)—The adventure, wit, poetry, and romance of *Cyrano de Bergerac* abound in Jean-Paul Rappeneau's robust new version from France. It stars Gerard Depardieu, who has never been more entertaining and engrossing. Considered the most popular character of the French stage since the debut of Edmond Rostand's play in 1898, *Cyrano de Bergerac* remains the eloquent symbol of romantic yearning and the purity of love, and that reputation will only be heightened by this wonderful film. 138 mins. ★★★★

Dances With Wolves (PG-13)—Kevin Costner's superb epic about the American frontier, and the best film ever made about Native Americans. A most impressive first-time director, Costner fills the screen with magnificent visual imagery and enough story and character to more than account for the film's exceptional running time. This may be a classic. 190 mins. ★★★★

Edward Scissorhands (PG-13)—This is a charming, bittersweet fable for the '90s, an inventive, symbolic tale of a most unusual hero, created by offbeat director Tim Burton. Edward (Johnny Depp) is a sadly isolated android, a robot boy whose kind heart and artistic soul are challenged by a dire handicap: He has razor-sharp scissors for hands. Winona Ryder, Dianne Wiest, Alan Arkin and Vincent Price co-star. 98 mins. ★★★★

Movie capsules

Capsulized reviews by **Jack Garner,** *Democrat and Chronicle* film critic, provide a guide to movies playing at area theaters. Ratings guide: ★★★★ Excellent ★★★ Good ★★ Fair ★ Poor.

Awakenings (PG-13)—Robert De Niro and Robin Williams star as a patient and a doctor in Penny Marshall's engrossing new film about a real-life medical miracle that proved as startling as it was ephemeral. The film is based on the highly regarded book by Oliver Sacks, a neurologist who unlocked the mysteries of an unusual disease that had left its victims frozen in a near-vegetative state for decades. Julie Kavner and Penelope Ann Miller co-star. The results include two of the most impressive performances of 1990 in a warmly entertaining and enlightening drama. 121 mins. ★★★★

Home Alone (PG-13)—To describe the setup of the latest John Hughes comedy is simplicity itself: A large family goes on a holiday vacation to Paris and inadvertently leaves one kid home alone for Christmas. But the boy shows remarkable resourcefulness and protects the home from two greedy burglars. Joe Pesci, Daniel Stern and a remarkable youngster named Macaulay Culkin co-star. Hughes' script has been directed by Chris Columbus. 98 mins. ★★★

Kindergarten Cop (PG-13)—The *Twins* team of Arnold Schwarzenegger and Director Ivan Reitman are back with another action-comedy, obviously designed to play off Arnold's good-natured comic sensibilities, and soften his action-hero image. Though a bit too obviously contrived, *Kindergarten Cop* is entertaining and funny and should please both Schwarzenegger's longtime action fans, and his new-found *Twins* following. Arnold plays a tough LA cop who goes undercover as a kindergarten teacher and discovers a whole new level of challenges. Note: Despite an obvious built-in appeal for youngsters, this film is justifiably rated PG-13. It may be about pre-schoolers, in part, but it's not designed for them. Pamela Reed, Penelope Ann Miller, Linda Hunt and Richard Tyson co-star. 110 mins. ★★★

Reprinted with permission of the *Times-Union* and *Democrat and Chronicle*, Rochester, NY (April 14, 1991), 10D.

Misery (R)—In the hands of capable director Rob Reiner, this is one of very few commendable Stephen King movie adaptations, and about as close as King's material may ever come to an Alfred Hitchcock movie. As a kidnapped writer, James Caan delivers his most engrossing performance since his memorable Sonny Corleone in *The Godfather*. Kathy Bates is equally effective as the writer's demented kidnapper, tormentor and self-described "No. 1 fan." 100 mins. ★★★

Cinema scope

Capsule plots of current movies, compiled by Will Astor.

Awakenings (PG-13): Robert De Niro plays a man who has spent 30 years in a catatonic semi-coma. Robin Williams is the doctor who brings him back. Question: Robin Williams? Answer: The doctor is described as "eccentric." The movie is described as drama. *General Cinema Marketplace (272-1470); General Cinema Pittsford Plaza (383-8855).*

Dances With Wolves (PG-13): Another step in Hollywood's contemporary revision of how the West was won. An American army officer (Kevin Costner) is assigned to a deserted fort during the Civil War. He befriends the local Lakota Sioux and is ultimately adopted into the tribe. He even gets to have a romance with a white woman who was conveniently adopted by the Sioux as a child. Costner directed. *Hoyts Cine Greece (225-3190); Jo-Mor's Eastview (223-3770); Loews Towne (424-4520); Loews Webster (671-6900).*

Green Card (PG-13): Gerard Depardieu stars in his first American movie, playing George Faure, a Frenchman who needs a Green Card so he can take a job in the United States. Andie Mac Dowell plays a woman who has just found the perfect New York City apartment. The only catch is that it's available only to a married couple. The rest isn't hard to imagine. *Jo-Mor's Stoneridge (371-7880); General Cinema Pittsford Plaza (383-8855).*

Home Alone (PG-13): A comedy from teen-flick maven John Hughes ("The Breakfast Club," "Pretty in Pink"). A 7-year-old boy is accidentally left behind while his parents vacation in Europe. Home alone (get it?), the boy has to cope with burglars and assorted crises. Sounds like a plausible premise. *Hoyts Cine Greece (225-3190); Loews Webster (671-6900); General Cinema Marketplace (272-1470); General Cinema Pittsford Plaza (383-8855).*

New Jack City (R): Streetwise cops go deep undercover to bring down a Harlem drug kingpin. Yo! Check it out! They're way past def and beyond stoopid. They're "new jack." No dis, etc. Mario Van Peebles directed and plays one of the cops. Ice-T and Judd Nelson round out the team. Wesley Snipes (the guy who shook his finger at Michael Jackson in the "Bad" video) is the homie-mobster, Nino Brown. *Loews Ridge (Opens Mar. 8, 865-5650); Loews Webster (Opens Mar. 8, 671-6900).*

The Silence of the Lambs (R): Jodie Foster plays an FBI agent-trainee on the trail of a demented killer. Her search leads her to Dr. Hannibal "the Cannibal" (Anthony Hopkins), a demented but brilliant psychiatrist, the only one who can lead her to the twisted murderer. *Hoyts Cine Greece (225-3190); Jo-Mor's Eastview (223-3770); Loews Pittsford (586-2900); Loews Webster (671-6900).*

Sleeping with the Enemy (R): Julia Roberts stars as a young woman whose four-year marriage appears ideal. But appearances are deceiving. She has to take desperate measures to get out of the destructive relationship. *Jo-Mor's Stoneridge (381-7880); Loews Webster (671-6900); General Cinema Marketplace (272-1470); General Cinema Pittsford Plaza (383-8855).*

White Fang (PG): Based on the Jack London novel. Two miners and their wolf-dog, White Fang, face natural and human perils in Alaska while staking out a claim. *Hoyts Cine Greece (225-3190); Jo-Mor's Eastview (223-3770); Loews Webster (671-6900).*

Notice that reviewers don't always agree with each other. One reviewer may like a movie, and another may hate the same movie. It's OK for people to have different opinions. After all, not everyone likes the same things.

Some critics use stars to indicate how much they liked a movie. (One star means *poor* and five stars mean *excellent.*) Others use numbers from 1 to 10, and still others use symbols of their own invention. Look at the summary below of how different newspaper reviewers feel about movies. Notice that some reviewers like a movie and others dislike it. Which movie below did the reviewers like the most? Which two movies were liked the least?

Develop your own symbols or rating system to indicate approval and disapproval of movies. Then draw a chart for the movies you have seen.

SNAP JUDGMENTS

Critics' views of current films, compiled by Will Astor.

	City	Times-Union	D&C	N.Y. Times	Newsweek	New Yorker	Village Voice	New York
Awakenings			seal of approval	a stinker		mixed reviews	a stinker	mixed reviews
The Field		seal of approval		mixed reviews			seal of approval	a stinker
Hamlet	a stinker	seal of approval	mixed reviews	seal of approval	seal of approval		mixed reviews	mixed reviews
He Said, She Said		mixed reviews		a stinker			mixed reviews	
King Ralph		mixed reviews		mixed reviews			mixed reviews	a stinker
L.A. Story		seal of approval		mixed reviews		mixed reviews	mixed reviews	mixed reviews
Mr. & Mrs. Bridge		a stinker	seal of approval	seal of approval		mixed reviews	seal of approval	seal of approval
Scenes from a Mall	a stinker	a stinker		mixed reviews			a stinker	mixed reviews
The Silence of the Lambs	seal of approval	seal of approval	seal of approval	seal of approval	seal of approval		seal of approval	seal of approval
Sleeping with the Enemy	a stinker	mixed reviews	mixed reviews		a stinker		seal of approval	a stinker

(seal) = seal of approval (mixed) = mixed reviews (skunk) = a stinker

Discussion Questions

1. Look back at the movie reviews given on the previous pages. Choose one that describes a movie that you have seen. Do you agree with the review? Why or why not?
2. If you had written the review, what would you have added?
3. Choose two reviews of the same movie and compare them. What differences do you see? What similarities do you see?
4. What types of things do movie reviews generally discuss?
5. What different types of movies are there? Name them and be prepared to explain what each is. Some have been listed for you.

   mystery
   horror
   western (cowboy)
   adventure

6. Which type of movie do you prefer, and why?
7. For each category listed in question number 5, name a movie that fits that description.
8. Look at a review of a movie that received strong approval, and compare it with a review that got one star or less.

Analyzing Student Movie Reviews

Below are two reviews written by students. Read the reviews and then answer the questions that follow.

Good flick

Yoav Rubin

I was in Loews Webster cinema which is a big theater with twelve screens. The movie that I saw was called "The Bonfire of the Vanities" with Bruce Willis, Melanie Griffith and Tom Hanks.

They are good actors. This movie is based on the Tom Wolfe novel about New York city yuppies. The hero is Sherman McCoy, a dealer on the stock exchange in a high position. One day he ran away from his home to meet his mistress when she arrived at a Kennedy Airport. They went over a bridge and got lost in the South Bronx, a dangerous area. It seemed as if they were going to be ambushed by two young Black people. One young man was run over by Sherman's car. Now the story began. I won't finish the story, but you must go to see it. "Bonfire of the Vanities" is a beautiful movie with a lot of humor. I recommend this movie.

Edward Scissorhands: a romantic fairy tale

Kuo-Chin-Mei

"Edward Scissorhands" is a romantic movie. The plot is very simple. However, the scenery is full of imagination and originality and this is the best part.

In this modern fairy tale, there is a boy called Edward, who was a man-like robot created by an inventor who died before he finished, and Edward was left with scissors for his hands. A local neighbor finds him and brings him home with her. Everyone in this residential area soon finds out how incredible and interesting Edward is, and he is popular until he is caught by the police. Before that happens, he falls in love with a young girl who is the daughter of the local neighbor who brought him home. Edward feels deeply hurt because he doesn't have normal hands, and he could hurt others, even himself, with his scissorhands. He realizes that it is impossible for him to have a normal relationship with the girl. So, he goes back to the place where he lived before.

The plot is just like "E.T." When people discover someone who is different from them or abnormal, some people over protect them and some just want to use them without caring about the feeling they have.

In the movie, Edward is played by Johnny Depp. He performs wonderfully in this movie. Anyway, this is a movie for those people who want to escape from reality. Also, it can satisfy those people who like visual art. I enjoyed it very much, and I think you will too!

Reprinted, by permission, from *The International Student News*, Rochester Institute of Technology.

Discussion Questions

1. What kind of movie is *Edward Scissorhands?*
2. What does the student reviewer like best about the movie?
3. How does the student's review compare with the professional movie reviewer's comments given earlier?
4. What is special about the main character?
5. What is the movie *The Bonfire of the Vanities* based on?
6. Who is the hero? What does he do?
7. Where does the movie take place?
8. What is the plot or story?
9. Does the student reviewer like the movie?
10. How does the student's review compare with the professional movie reviewer's comments given earlier?

Thinking about Movies

When people leave a movie theater, they usually discuss the movie. They talk about what they liked and disliked. They talk about the acting, the story, the funny and sad parts. They may compare it to another movie that they have seen on a similar subject. They may remember a particular scene they liked because it was funny, touching, or scary. If someone asks them about the movie, they are prepared to give a review although that is not what they would call it.

What movies have you seen recently? Did you like them? Why or why not?

Use the chart below to help you think about some of the important aspects of reviewing a movie, and fill in the chart for a movie that you have seen. Then answer the questions that follow.

Name of Movie ______________________________

Type of movie ______________________________

Plot

____

____

____

____

____

____

Characters (describe at least two).

____

____

____

____

____

____

Acting (name two one or two actors and discuss their acting).

____

____

____

____

____

____

Favorite scene (choose a scene that you liked the best, describe it, and tell why you liked it).

______

______

______

______

______

______

WRITING MOVIE REVIEWS EXERCISE 1

In this exercise, you will write a review of a movie. Follow the guide questions below, which will help you to prepare your review.

1. What is the name of the movie you are going to review?

______

2. What kind of movie is it?

______

3. Did you like it? How many stars will you give it?

______

4. Who played leading roles in the movie? Did you like their performances? Why or why not?

______

______

______

5. What one scene do you remember because it was especially good or especially bad? Describe it.

______

______

______

6. What kind of audience will like this movie? Teenagers, children, adults?

____

7. What else was special about the movie? (The scenery? The music? The sound effects? The costumes? The script?)

____

____

____

8. What is your opinion of the story?

____

____

____

WRITING MOVIE REVIEWS EXERCISE 2

Part A

After you have answered the above questions, write your movie review. (Use a separate sheet of paper.) Be sure to introduce the movie to the reader in the first paragraph. Tell your opinion of it. Explain why you have this opinion. Discuss other important features, and give the movie an appropriate number of stars. You may, if you wish, use one of the previous reviews as a model.

WRITING MOVIE REVIEWS EXERCISE 2

Part B

Exchange papers with another student. Read each other's reviews. Has the writer answered all the questions you wanted to have answered? Use the guide questions as a check. Write down any suggestions that you have for the reviewer.

Does the review make you interested in seeing this movie? Why or why not?

Return papers and make any necessary changes based on the reader's recommendations.

Writing Television Reviews

Your teacher may assign you as a class to see a particular television show or divide the class into groups and assign each group a different television show to watch.

As you watch television, use these questions as a guide in preparation for writing a review. Write your answers below.

1. What is the name of the show you watched?

____

2. What time did the show appear, and what station was it on?

____

3. What type of show was it?

____

4. Were the performers/actors good? Who were they? What made their performances good or poor?

____

____

____

5. How many stars would you give this show? (Remember one star means *poor* and five means *excellent.*)

____

Note that the questions given above are general. The class or each group should develop its own set of questions to fit the type of show that they will be watching.

Group Guide Questions

1. ______________________________
2. ______________________________
3. ______________________________
4. ______________________________
5. ______________________________

After you have viewed the show, compare your answers to the questions with your classmates' responses. Did some people have different answers? If so, discuss why. Did some people give the show one star and others four stars? Discuss why people liked or disliked the show.

After these steps, your teacher may have you write a joint review of the show, or he or she may assign you to write a review of your own. Give the television show an appropriate number of stars. Be prepared to share your review with the rest of the class.

Writing Restaurant Reviews

Just as movies, television shows, and plays can be reviewed, so can restaurants. When we review a movie, we think of the plot, the characters, and the acting. When we review a restaurant, we consider whether the food was tasty and hot. We consider the cost, the service, the courtesy, and the atmosphere. Read the restaurant reviews below and then answer the questions that follow.

Restaurants

Hong Kong is justly famous for its food, and indeed is a place where dining out is the preferred form of eating because prices here are much less expensive than their New York counterparts. It is advisable to make reservations.

For a splurge, and a taste of Cantonese haute cuisine, try the elegant Man Wah Restaurant atop the Mandarin Hotel (522-0111). Special winter dishes include braised supreme snake soup ($11.50 per bowl) and a wintry hot pot that the restaurant calls Chinese fondue. That meal features 13 ingredients, including fresh prawns, scallops, crab claw and fresh vegetables, which you cook at your table, dipping them into a pot of hot broth, and costs $36 per person. Dinner for two with a glass of wine runs to about $70.

Cleveland Sichuan (6 Cleveland Street, Causeway Bay; 576-3876) is a comfortable restaurant with good spicy food and a number of sizzling dishes that the local Chinese love—hot, hot metal platters of fish, meat or chicken that sizzle and smoke when doused in a sauce. The sizzling beef with spring onions and garlic is excellent. Dinner for two with drinks about $50.

Another fine Sichuan restaurant is the Red Pepper (7 Lan Fong Road, Causeway Bay; 576-8046) a plain, family run eatery with good spicy food like eggplant with hot garlic sauce, and chili and garlic prawns. Dinner for two with drinks about $40.

Spring Deer (42 Mody Road, Kowloon; 366-4012) is a homey, second-floor Peking restaurant justly noted for its delicious Peking Duck, which can be ordered on the spot. Dinner for two with drinks about $45.

Sun Hung Cheung Hing (45A Kimberley Road, Kowloon; 369-3435) is a real working-class restaurant that offers a Mongolian barbecue. Each table is equipped with a big metal hot plate. Order plates of chicken, beef and squid and prawns. They come with a half-dozen small plates of fresh vegetables, together with coriander, leeks and spring onions, great spicy barbecue sauce, soy sauce and oil. Pour oil on the hot plate, dip the meat in the sauce and throw it on the hot plate with the vegetables. Dinner for two with drinks about $25.

Reprinted, by permission, from *The New York Times* (August 13, 1991).

Restaurant review
Win some, lose some at inconsistent Dac Hoa

By Patrick Farrell

The first time I ate at Dac Hoa Restaurant, a few weeks ago, a fight broke out in the kitchen and one of the cooks was knifed in the arm.

I mention this not to alarm anybody; the scuffle was brief, there was a doctor in the house, and the two waitresses handled the situation with admirable poise. But after it was over, the whole incident made me wish that the kitchen staff would save some of that passion for their food.

Dac Hoa is a Vietnamese/Chinese restaurant that moved about four months ago into the Monroe Avenue storefront across from the former Sears building that used to house the Saigon, another Vietnamese restaurant that's reopened at Gregory Street and South Clinton Avenue as Kim's Asia Restaurant. You may know Dac Hoa as the place that displays roast ducks and pig heads in the window, like Oriental eateries in New York City or Toronto.

That big-city feel continues inside; the newly remodeled room has a modern, almost cafeteria-like look. Even the plates and chopsticks are plastic. Service is incredibly quick, and perhaps too quick, because some of the food tastes as if it were prepared earlier and then quickly, unevenly, reheated — if at all. On two different visits, tea and soup arrived lukewarm.

The menu is large, with Chinese dishes far outnumbering the Vietnamese, as they often do in restaurants that modify their cuisine for American tastes. But that's not the case here — for better *and* worse. In a Westernized restaurant, you wouldn't find anything as subtly complex as the tangy beef noodle soup ($4), a broth spiced with cinnamon and basil, with beef strips, beef balls and vermicelli, and garnished with lime and fresh bean sprouts for you to throw in. Nor could you try anything as unusual as the rice pastry with sausage ($3.50), a sticy translucent dough filled with ground meat and piled with sprouts and bits of fried onion. Then again, you may not *want* anything as unusual as the slices of pressed mystery meat that top the rice pastry, or the gummy, clear sauce on what might have been a simple plate of crisp fried vegetables ($4.95).

But what ultimately disappoints at Dac Hoa is the blandness of so much of the food. Spring rolls (two for $1.99) had the standard glut of lettuce, a little diced beef, a few shrimp and a light, fresh warpper, but no seasoning to lend them any spring. The egg rolls (same price) were needlessly greasy.

Chicken Hunan style ($5.75) sported a brown sauce, with no discernible flavor, over peapods and baby corn cobs that had been stir-fried into submission. Lured by the window display, I tried the duck with spicy salt ($8.95). The black-pepper coating was fiery but sparsely applied, and most of the bird was dry and tough, as if it had spent too many long evenings gazing out at Monroe Avenue.

And yet this place can produce something as snappy as the beef with black bean sauce ($5.50). The beef strips were lean and cooked just to tenderness, like the bell peppers and onions. The sauce could have used less cornstarch, but it was sharp with hot pepper and didn't skimp on the black beans.

Are a good chef and a bad chef battling it out in the kitchen? If so, until one or the other prevails, your chances here are likely to be hit-or-miss.

Patrick Farrel is a Times-Union *staff member.*

Discussion Questions

1. What does the first paragraph of each review tell the reader?

___

___

___

2. What interesting information appears in the second paragraph of the Dac Hoa restaurant?

___

___

___

3. The first review discusses five restaurants. Does the reviewer provide the reader with the same type of information in each review? If so, what type of information is the same? If not, what is different?

___

___

___

4. Which of the five restaurants described in the first review would you prefer to go to? Explain why.

___

___

___

5. What is unusual about the way the review of the Dac Hoa restaurant is written?

____

____

____

6. Would you like to eat at the Dac Hoa restaurant? Why or why not?

____

____

____

7. Which of the restaurant reviews offers the most in the way of reviewer opinion? Which form of review do you prefer?

____

____

____

8. The Dac Hoa review gives a letter grade of C−. What does that mean?

____

____

____

Analyzing Student Restaurant Reviews

Below are two restaurant reviews that have been written by students. Read them and then answer the questions that follow.

Food section
Junk food bigger, cheaper in U.S.A.

Kimiyo Fukuda

Many American people go to fast food restaurants. Why have the fast food restaurants permeated through the American society, and why were the fast food restaurants developed? There are several reasons why fast food restaurants are popular in the United States. One reason is because American like to go to restaurants with reasonable, low prices. Another reason is that they are busy, so they don't like to take time to cook food or eat it.

The fast food industry has developed rapidly, especially in this decade. After the fuse was lit in America, it spread to many countries. I don't know about fast food restaurants in other countries, so I will compare fast food restaurants in my country and the United States.

I went to Wendy's and Mc Donald's near the shopping mall during my holidays. Both of the restaurants had almost the same appearance and structure. As the restaurants had many windows, the bright sunshine poured in. The tables and the chairs were arranged not to stand in the customers' way. This is similar to Japan, too.

To my surprise, American regular size hamburgers are very big and cheap as compared to Japanese hamburgers. American regular size hamburgers are equal to large size hamburgers in Japan. In the United States, medium size drinks and other foods are also bigger than in Japan. This maybe because Americans are heavy eaters, or it maybe because food is cheaper in America than in Japan.

The food in American fast food restaurants tastes different than in Japan. I think American meat is fresher and juicier. Coca Cola and French fries are almost the same both in Japan and America.

Now, the fast food industry has become very popular and they compete with other companies. They compete about price, taste and service against their rivals, so they want to gain customers' confidence. We can choose our favorite fast food restaurants from many possibilities in Japan and America.

Reprinted, by permission, from *The International Student News*, Rochester Institute of Technology (February 1991).

Best restaurant in Rochester

Suk Won Ha

I have visited a lot of restaurants and bars. Some places are very expensive and the others are not. Usually expensive restaurants are decorated with luxurious stuff, but they are not always loved by customers. Even if some restaurants are not luxurious, many people like those places.

Last summer, I went to the Mandarin Palace which is a Chinese restaurant for the the first time. The Mandarin looks like a normal Chinese restaurant. There are two gates before you get inside. The Mandarin consists of three sections and one bar, and some traditional Chinese pictures are hung on the wall. When I visited the Mandarin first, I just thought it was a good place, so I visited pretty often. I liked the Mandarin more and more because there was a very familiar atmosphere.

Jing is a Chinese who manages the Mandarin. He is also a very nice guy. He had been in Korea for fifteen years, so he can speak Korean perfectly. He is very close with customers. Whether customers are old people or young people, he talks with them like a friend, so everybody likes him.

There is also a nice cook. The Mandarin has almost one hundred fifteen different kinds of food, and each food has a special taste. The food is pretty cheap and tastes nice. Not only Asian people like the Mandarin's food, but Americans also do. Jing's parents work in the kitchen, they are very experienced cooks.

The Mandarin is the best restaurant in Rochester. Of course, it is my opinion, but if you go there, you will have the same opinion as mine. I want to recommend it to you, and I guarantee you will like it.

Reprinted, by permission, from *The International Student News*, Rochester Institute of Technology (February 1991).

Discussion Questions

1. What are fast food restaurants? Why does the first reviewer begin by talking about them?
2. What surprised the first reviewer about McDonald's food in the United States and in Japan?
3. What does the second reviewer like about the Mandarin restaurant?
4. What kind of atmosphere does the Mandarin restaurant have?

WRITING A RESTAURANT REVIEW

Your teacher may divide the class into groups of three or four. Each group has as its assignment to go to a restaurant and write a review.

When you go to the restaurant, be sure to take notes. Use the following questions as a guide. Add any other information that you feel is important.

Guide Questions

1. What is the restaurant like? Describe the atmosphere, decorations, colors, noise, etc.

   ___

2. What type of restaurant is it? Is it a fast food restaurant? A fancy restaurant? What are the prices? Are they fair for what you were getting?

   ___

3. How is the food? Consider the following.

   What did you eat? Describe it.
   How much did it cost?
   Was it tasty?
   What ingredients could you taste?
   How did the dish you ordered compare to the same dish prepared in other restaurants?
   How did the quality of the food (in general) compare to food at other similar restaurants?

   ___

   ___

   ___

   ___

4. How was the service? Too slow? Too fast?

   ___

5. What grade would you give the restaurant?

____

6. What other important information should you discuss?

____

Writing Your Restaurant Review

Write a short review of the restaurant, using the space provided below.

Name of restaurant _______________________________

Chapter 9

Writing Letters and Memos

The goals for this chapter are:

To learn the format for various types of correspondence

- notes
- memos
- friendly letters
- formal letters

To use summarizing techniques

To use guided writing

Would you speak to your teacher, your boss, or the president of a company the same way that you speak to a friend? No, of course not. Is conversation in the locker room or on the athletic field different from conversation in the classroom? What is different? Consider the following areas, and identify how they would be different depending upon whom you were speaking to or where you were.

vocabulary
style
formality
tone
grammar

Just as we change our speech depending on whom we are talking to, we also change the way we write depending upon whom we are writing to.

If we are writing a short note to a friend, it will be different from a letter in which we ask for a job. A letter to a parent will be different from a letter written to a company in order to buy something. Information sent from one employee to another within a company may be sent as a memo instead of as a letter.

In this chapter, we will discuss the different types of letters people write and their forms.

Writing a Simple Note

Simple notes are informal. They are usually the kind of notes we do not mail. They are notes we leave on a friend's desk or under the door if someone isn't home. They are the kind of note we might put in a teacher's mailbox at school to tell her we are going home sick and won't be in class. We write them to tell someone we know some important information. Simple notes are usually very short and to the point.

For example, look at the following and the note that a friend sent to his classmate.

Bicycle for sale

Ten-speed bicycle for sale. Good condition. Only one year old. $40. Call 475-9980.

Dear Jerry,

There is an ad in yesterday's newspaper that I thought you would be interested in. Someone is selling a ten-speed bike for $40! I know you are looking for a bike, so I thought I would tell you about it. If you are interested, call 475-9980. Good luck.

Your classmate,

Tom

Jerry also got a letter from Susan. She wrote:

Hi Jerry,

Someone is selling a ten-speed bike for $40. Sounds like a good deal. Thought you might be interested.

Sue

(Notice that in Susan's note she omitted the subject "it" in the second sentence and the subject "I" in the third sentence. In an informal note, this is acceptable when the subject is understood.

NOTE-WRITING EXERCISE

Now that you have seen some examples of how to write notes and how to summarize the information in an ad, try writing one or two notes of your own. Below are some classified ads from the newspaper. Some are ads in which people are selling things, others are ads for apartments for rent, and still others are ads for jobs. Read the following ads, and write a note (use a separate sheet of paper) to one or two of your classmates telling them about one of the ads.

For sale

27" Color TV. Good condition. $75. Call 221-6689.
Small, dormitory-size refrigerator. $25. Call Stan, 333-3453.
1989 Ford Mustang. Excellent condition. $5,550. Call 444-875.
CD player. Excellent condition. Must sell. $100. Call 221-1122.

Part-time jobs

Translator: many languages needed. Good pay. Call 989-0066.

Dishwasher: nights. Good pay. Come to Mama's Pizza Place, 466 Melbourne.

Babysitter needed. Tuesdays 9 A.M.–5 P.M. for two children. $40 per day. Call Robert, 761-1879.

WRITING MESSAGES EXERCISE 1

Taking a message is also a form of note writing. Read the telephone conversation below. Then write a message for David.

(Telephone rings.)
You: Hello.
Caller: Hi. Is David there?
You: No, he's not. Can I take a message?
Caller: Yes. Please tell him that Susan called. Tell him that I can't meet him at the library tomorrow at noon. I forgot that I have a dentist's appointment. Oh, tell him that I'm sorry. Also, remind him to drop off my calculus book by Tuesday evening. My exam is Thursday. By the way, how is his mother? I heard she was in the hospital.
You: She's fine. I'll tell him you called.

Write Your Message Here

____

____

____

WRITING MESSAGES EXERCISE 2

Leave a message for Jennifer.

(Telephone rings.)
You: Hello. This is Amrack and Aldridge, Counselors-at-Law.
Caller: Hello. I need to speak with Jennifer Capers right away.
You: I'm sorry, she's not in. Can I take a message for her?
Caller: Yes, tell her Jaime Bennington called. The bank won't give me the loan. If I can't get the loan, will I have to take a second mortgage on my house? Also, I need to know what the accountant said when he checked the books of the company I want to buy. Tell her this is an emergency, and she has to get back to me immediately. I need to find some kind of interim loan if this deal is going to happen.
You: I'll leave her your message.
Caller: Thank you. Good-bye.

Write Your Message Here

WRITING MESSAGES EXERCISE 3

(Telephone rings.)

You: Hello.

Caller: Hello. This is Randy McFirst calling from International Associates. May I speak with Stephen Drake?

You: He's not in. Can I take a message?

Caller: Yes, please. Tell Stephen that we were impressed with him at the interview last week, and we would like him to send us the names and addresses of three references. We'd like one to be from an employer, one to be from a teacher, and one to be from someone who knows him well, but not a family member.

You: I'll tell him.

Caller: Please also tell him we will need to have the letters of reference by a week from Tuesday, and they should be sent directly to my attention. Also, he'll need to call my secretary to set up an appointment for a second round of interviews. Have him call as soon as possible.

You: OK. I will.

Write Your Message Here

WRITING MESSAGES EXERCISE 4

In chapter 6, you read a radio play about Mrs. Stevenson. Go back to that chapter. Do you remember the story? Reread it if you have forgotten it. Now, pretend that you are one of the following people, and on a separate sheet of paper, write a message according to the instructions below. Then answer the questions that follow.

1. You are the operator whom Mrs. Stevenson calls to tell about the murder that she heard two men planning. Write a message for the next operator who will take your place when you go off work. Tell her about the lady who called today.
2. You are the policeman whom Mrs. Stevenson calls. Write a message for your boss about the telephone call you received.
3. You are Mrs. Stevenson. The phone downstairs has just clicked. You know that the murderer is in the house and he is after you. Write a message for the police to find in case you are murdered.
4. You are Mrs. Stevenson. You have just figured out that your husband has paid someone to kill you. Write a message to your husband!

Discussion Questions

Read to the class some of the messages students have written.

1. How are the messages similar?
2. How are they different?
3. What different feelings do people convey in their messages? How do they get these different feelings across?
4. Did anyone in the class write an angry message? Read some angry messages. How do you know they are angry? What kind of language do they use?
5. Did anyone in the class write a sad message? Read some sad messages. How do you know they are sad? What kind of language do they use?

Memo

To: (name of the person the memo is going to)

From: (your name)

Date: (the date)

Subject: (the purpose of the memo)

(The memo goes in this space.)

____

____

____

____

____

Writing Memos

People who work for the same company or organization usually write memos to each other instead of letters. The word *memo* stands for *memorandum.* A memo is usually short and to the point. It is written for a very busy person who doesn't have much time to read it. For this reason, all the important information is in the beginning of the memo, and the memo is as short as possible. Note the format for writing a memo on page 168.

After the memo has been typed, sign it next to your name at the top where it says "From."

Purpose of Memos

People write memos to provide and ask for information, and to make recommendations. For example, in the first exercise in this chapter, you wrote notes to classmates to inform them of something you saw advertised in the newspaper. That type of writing is informal and personal.

A memo is used in the workplace; therefore, it is more formal. Most companies have preprinted memo forms onto which people can write or type their memos.

WRITING MEMOS EXERCISE 1

Imagine that your company has sent you to attend this English class and that you are expected to write a memo to your boss upon your return. Your memo must discuss the English class you participated in, rate it, and let the boss know whether you would recommend that the company send other people to this class. Think about what you might say. What have you learned? What were the positive and negative aspects of the class? Is what you learned going to help you on the job in the future?

Jot some notes in the space below and use a separate sheet of paper to complete your memo.

Memo

To: ______________________________

From: ______________________________

Date: ______________________________

Subject: ______________________________

____

____

____

____

WRITING MEMOS EXERCISE 2

Imagine that you work for an architectural firm. Your firm has been working on a project to design a building that will be taller than the 110-story Sears Tower in Chicago.

You have just read the information below. You think it is important that the people in your company who are working on this project know about the project being considered in Japan. Send a memo to a fellow employee informing her of this article.

Write your memo on a separate sheet of paper.

500-story Tokyo building would resist earthquakes.

500-Story Tokyo building would hold 300,000 people $326.2 Billion structure would take 25 years to construct

The Associated Press

TOKYO—A construction company said yesterday it has designed a 500-story skyscraper for Tokyo although there are no immediate plans to build it.

The designers would need 25 years and $326.2 billion to build the 6,669-foot-tall Aeropolis 2001, said Yasuyuki Kimura, a spokesman for Ohbayashi Corp.

This includes the money necessary to reclaim a 56-square-mile island in Tokyo Bay, he added.

The project was made possible by Japan's advanced techniques to protect buildings in earthquakes, he said.

The tallest building in earthquake-prone Japan is the 60-story Sunshine City Building in Tokyo. The 110-story Sears Tower in Chicago is the world's tallest building.

Yukihisa Tokunaga, a city planning official of the Construction Ministry, said the 500-story building is one of a number of private plans by major construction firms to meet Tokyo's growing need for office and apartment space.

"I understand that none of the plans, including what they call 'Waterfronts,' 'Geofronts,' 'Undergroundpolis' and 'Aeropolis,' has been submitted for any government approval," Tokunaga said.

The Ohbayashi building would be able to accommodate 300,000 people. Aside from office space and residential units, it also would have space for hotels, hospitals, parks and convention centers.

The design envisions elevators that would reach the top floor in 15 minutes.

The building is shaped like a triangle, becoming smaller at the top to help it absorb shock waves. It would have a number of tunnels to let typhoon winds pass through rather than hitting the building with full force.

The Japanese archipelago, in the world's most active seismic zone, is hit each year by some 1,000 tremors strong enough to be felt. Three times this century, in 1923, 1946 and 1948, quake deaths have climbed into the thousands. The Great Kanto Earthquake of 1923 leveled vast areas of Tokyo and Yokohama, killing 140,000 people.

About 25 typhoons develop in the region annually.

Writing Friendly Letters

We write friendly letters to people we know. We write friendly letters to relatives and to friends; these letters are usually informal, and they often have a conversational tone. A friendly letter is a very common form of writing and often the form that students feel most comfortable writing. It is usually a chatty letter that talks about things that are happening or have happened in the writer's life. In English, the form of a friendly letter is as follows:

Date

Dear (first name),

____

____

____

____

____

Sincerely,
Love,
Fondly,
Your friend,

} (Choose one of these closings depending on your relationship to the person.)

WRITING A FRIENDLY LETTER

Write a friendly letter to someone. Tell the person what you have been doing recently. Use a separate sheet of paper.

Writing Formal Letters

Formal letters are different from informal letters. The language is not chatty; it is formal and to the point. We write formal letters to order items from a company, to ask for a job interview, to request an application, to complain about a product, to request information, and so forth.

Below is the format used in a business letter. (Business letters should be typed.)

(your street address)
(your city, state, and zip code)
(the date)

(the name of the person or company you are writing to)
(the person's or company's street address)
(the person or company's city, state, and zip code)

Dear (the person's title (Mr., Mrs., Ms., Dr., Professor, etc.) and last name):

(If you do not know a person's name you may say To whom it may concern:)

(In the body of the letter, do not indent as you do when you write in longhand. Simply skip a line between paragraphs.)

Sincerely yours,
Very truly yours,
Yours truly,
Sincerely,
} (choose one)

(your signature)

(your name typed)

WRITING FORMAL LETTERS EXERCISE 1

Think of a city you would like to visit. Write a letter to the Chamber of Commerce in that city asking them to send you information about the city. Go to the library and get the address of the Chamber of Commerce in that city, and then mail your letter.

WRITING FORMAL LETTERS EXERCISE 2

Think of a university you would like to attend in the United States. Write a letter to the Admissions Office. Ask them to send you an application and a catalogue of the courses they offer. Be sure to tell them what subject you are interested in studying and whether you want to study at the graduate or undergraduate level.

Write your letter on a separate sheet of paper.

WRITING FORMAL LETTERS EXERCISE 3

You have just received your telephone bill. The Call It telephone company has charged you fifty dollars for a call to Iceland. You do not know anyone in Iceland. Write the telephone company a letter, and tell them about the situation. Ask them to remove the charge from your bill. Their address is:

Call It Phone Company
188 Long Distance Street
Boca Raton, FL 33433

Guide Questions

1. Why are you writing this letter?

____

2. What is the problem you are trying to correct?

____

3. Have you ever been to Iceland? Do you know anyone in Iceland?

____

4. Are you going to pay for the telephone call?

____

5. What do you want the phone company to do about the charge?

____

6. What is your telephone number?

____

Write your letter on a separate sheet of paper.

WRITING FORMAL LETTERS EXERCISE 4

You have just received your Charge It credit card bill. There is an error. The company has charged you $2,590 for a fur coat that you did not buy. Write a letter to the credit card company explaining the problem and telling them that you are not going to pay the $2,590 bill because it is a mistake.

Guide Questions

1. Why are you writing this letter?

____

2. What is the problem you are trying to correct?

____

3. Are you going to pay the $2,590?

____

4. What do you want the company to do?

____

Write your letter on a separate sheet of paper.

Chapter 10

Writing Comparisons

The goals for this chapter are:

To use comparisons in writing

To learn words used in comparisons

To support conclusions by using comparisons

To extract information from comparison charts

- airline information
- exchange rate information
- housing information
- stock market information

To make recommendations

To use guided writing

We often compare things before making decisions. For example, when we go to the supermarket, we may pick up an apple, turn it over in our hand, and put it back. As we look for a better apple, we may check to see that there is no crack in the skin and no soft spot. We may want it to be very red and shiny. We may compare the price and the quality of different types of apples before we make our purchase.

We do the same thing when we shop for clothes, computers, cars, CD players, or airline tickets. We may compare ideas, philosophies, books, people, results of experiments, medications, teachers, styles, and so on. Generally, when we compare things, we come to a conclusion that one thing is better than another.

In this chapter, we will analyze information. We will compare different things, come to some conclusions, and write about why we have made a particular decision.

Thinking about Comparisons

Look at the drawing on page 177. What do you see in the box on the top? Describe it.

Now look at the box on the bottom. Describe it.

When you look at the two boxes together, are the lines in each box parallel? When you look at each box separately, are the lines in each box parallel?

Compare the two boxes. What "trick" is being used here to fool your eyes?

In this exercise, you were making comparisons and coming to conclusions. You determined which lines were parallel, and you knew why you had made that choice.

You may be wondering what these drawings have to do with writing. In many ways, drawing and writing are similar. Both drawing and writing communicate an idea to another person. If the lines of a drawing are unclear or the ideas in an essay are muddled, the other person cannot understand the message the artist or writer wishes to express. When we write, as when we draw, our idea or message must be understood. In a drawing, the lines must be clear; the image must be understood; there cannot be extra lines that confuse the viewer. Similarly, in a piece of writing, the sentences must be clear, and the idea must be understood; there can be no unnecessary information, no irrelevant ideas.

If the artist intends the viewer to see the pain of war and the viewer sees only a battlefield, communication has not occurred. The intended message has not been understood.

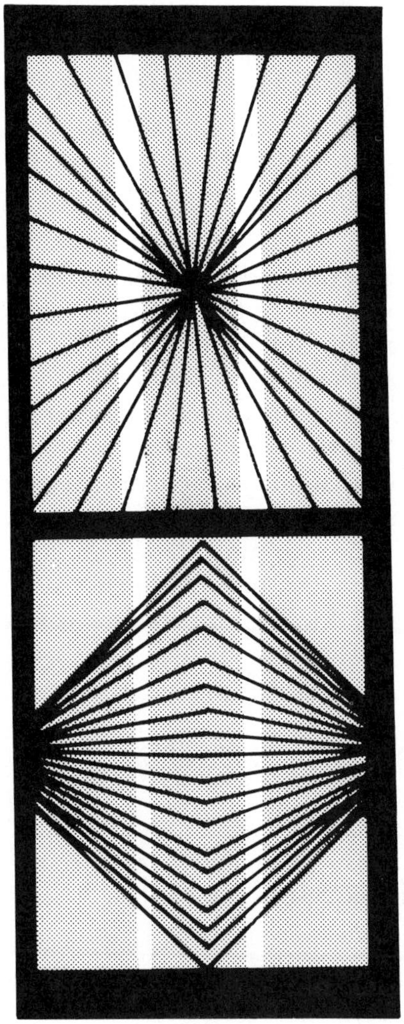

Are the two lines parallel? Reprinted, by permission, from Pierre Casse, *Training for the Cross Cultural Mind.*

This is true in all forms of writing, but often writers of comparison tend to spend too much time on each area, and the reader becomes confused. As a writer you must keep your purpose in mind and never lose sight of your focus.

In this chapter, we will compare things. As we make comparisons, we must remember to explain each of the ideas we are comparing so that the reader will understand the information. The exercise below provides a chart to assist you in the comparison process.

WRITING COMPARISONS EXERCISE 1

Pretend that you are a travel agent who has been asked to plan a trip by plane from Toronto, Canada, to Sydney, Australia. You must look at the information below and determine which airline to recommend and why.

After analyzing the information in the chart, you will need to write a letter in which you compare each of the airlines and recommend one to your customer.

Airline	*Cost*	*Departure*	*Arrival*	*Stopover*	*Change planes*
CANAIR	$650	7:15 P.M.	10:00 A.M.	4 hours	yes
AUSAIR	$845	7:15 P.M.	6:45 A.M.	nonstop	no
EXAIR	$2,465	2:00 P.M.	6:00 P.M.	nonstop	no

You know the cost of the flight. You also know how long the flight will take and whether or not there will be a stopover. You must decide which of these flights is more appropriate for your client. To do this, you must think about the audience (the client or customer).

Here are some questions to help you prepare a letter to your client:

1. What do you know about your client? (Make up a brief profile.) Be creative! Remember that the information about your audience or client will determine your recommendation and the content of your letter. Is your client very wealthy and in a hurry? Is she looking for the least expensive flight and doesn't care about inconvenience?

____

2. Based on what you know, which airline is the best choice for your client?

____

3. Give two or three reasons why you will recommend this one to your client.

a. ____________________________________

b. ____________________________________

c. ____________________________________

Now write a draft of a letter to your client. In your letter, recommend one of the airlines and explain why you think it is the best one for her. As you write your draft, use the questions below to help focus your ideas.

Guide Questions

1. What can you say in your first sentence to explain why you are writing this letter?

____

2. What are you recommending?

____

3. Why are you recommending this airline?

___

4. Why aren't you recommending the other two airlines?

___

5. What can you say at the end of the letter to encourage her to call you if she needs more information, or if she wants to make a reservation?

___

Write the finished version of your letter on a separate piece of paper.

Transitional Words for Comparisons

When we write an essay in which we are comparing things, we often use words that show comparison. These words are like the signs you see along a highway. They tell the reader what direction you, the writer, are going in. For example, if you want to say that two things are good but one of them is better, you can say:

Although Fly Right is a good airline, Wings Way is better.

Or you can say:

Fly Right is a good airline, *but* Wings Way is better.

If you want to remind the reader that you are comparing two things, you can say:

When we compare the two, it is important to remember the price.
Fly Right isn't the only good airline. Wings Way is *also* good.
Another similarity between them is their safety record.
Another difference between them is the quality of the food.
Both have good safety records.
While it is true that Wings Way was on strike last year, it appears to be operating without difficulty this year.
Wings Way is *also* a member of the pilots' union.

WRITING COMPARISONS EXERCISE 2

Look at the table on page 180 which provides the conversion rates for money around the world compared to the U.S. dollar. The first column shows the exchange rates as of November 4, 1991; the second column shows the exchange rates for November 4, 1990 (a year before).

Compare the change in the exchange rate for your native country for each of the dates listed on the charts. Did the value of your native country's money go up or down compared to the U.S. dollar over this time period? Next, look in a local newspaper to see what its value is today.

Now choose another country and do the same thing. How has the value of that country's money changed in comparison with the U.S. dollar over the same time period? What is the value of that country's money today?

Use the guide questions which follow to write about the differences in the exchange rate for your country and the other country over this period of time. (Use a separate sheet of paper to write your comparison.) In your essay explain where you would have gotten the most value for your money during this time period—in your native country, in the U.S., or in the other country you chose.

$1 Equals . . .

Rates paid to individual travelers in the United States for each dollar changed, minus service fees. Rates may be more favorable abroad, or for large businesses.

	Nov. 4, 1991	Year Ago
AFRICA		
Kenya (shilling)*	22.25	18.69
Morocco (dirham)*	8.31	7.79
Senegal (C.F.A. franc)	262.00	234.00
South Africa (rand)*	2.80	2.32
THE AMERICAS		
Argentina (austral)	8,929.00	4,975.00
Brazil (cruzeiro)	795.00	83.44
Canada (dollar)	1.05	1.10
Mexico (peso)	2,924 .00	2,695.00
ASIA PACIFIC		
Australia (dollar)	1.19	1.19
Hong Kong (dollar)	7.21	7.24
India (rupee)*	25.96	16.39
Japan (yen)	124.00	120.00
New Zealand (dollar)	1.64	1.52
EUROPE		
Austria (schilling)	10.65	9.72
Belgium (franc)	31.20	28.45
Britain (pound)	0.54	0.48
Denmark (krone)	5.90	5.32
France (franc)	5.35	4.66
Germany (mark)	1.57	1.40
Greece (drachma)*	168.00	139.00
Ireland (punt)	.58	.52
Italy (lira)	1,176.00	1,045.00
Portugal (escudo)	129.00	121.00
Spain (peseta)	98.00	87.32
Sweden (krona)	5.53	5.18
Switzerland (franc)	1.38	1.18
MIDDLE EAST		
Egypt (pound)*	2.75	2.22
Israel (shekel)	2.11	2.07
Turkey (lira)	4,065.00	2,336.00

*The import of bank notes by nonresidents is restricted or prohibited.

Source: *Thomas Cook Foreign Exchange*

Reprinted, by permission, from *The New York Times* (January 13, 1991).

Guide Questions

1. What is the name of the first currency that you checked?

____

2. What country uses this currency?

____

3. How much was the currency worth against the U.S. dollar on each of the two dates?

____

4. Did the value of the currency go up or down compared to the U.S. dollar?

---

5. What do you think the change indicates?

---

6. What other currency did you check?

---

7. What country uses this currency?

---

8. Compared to the first currency you checked, how did this currency do during the same time period?

---

9. How do the changes for each currency compare with each other?

---

10. What do you think these results demonstrate?

More Practice with Transitional Words for Comparisons

When we compare, we use connecting words. Connecting words show a link or connection between two ideas. For example, when we are talking about the currency of one country going up and another going down, we might say:

The pound went up during this time, *but* the lira went down.

We could also say:

While the pound went up, the lira went down.

Or we could say:

While the pound was going up, the lira was going down.

The pound went up, *but* the lira went down.

Or we could say:

The pound went up *although* the lira went down. *Although* the lira went down, the pound went up.

WRITING COMPARISONS EXERCISE 3

Below are three charts that reflect the lowest airfares for popular routes, the currency exchange rate, and the world weather at a particular time of year. Look at the three charts, and then write an essay indicating the best place to go at that time of year. Be prepared to explain your reasons.

TRAVEL WATCH

Lowest Air Fares for Popular Routes

The lowest restricted and unrestricted round-trip fares as of Monday, Nov. 4, for commonly traveled domestic and overseas air routes. Reserve promptly to meet advance-purchase requirements: availability is not assured.

	Discount Fare Airlines	Unrestricted Fare Airlines
DOMESTIC ROUTES / Dec. 1-7		
New York-Atlanta	$268: T.W.A.	$448: T.W.A.
New York-Chicago	$198: American, Continental, Midway, T.W.A., United	$318: Midway
New York-Denver	$248: American, Continental, T.W.A, United	$550: T.W.A.
New York-Phoenix	$285: T.W.A.	$418: America West
New York-San Francisco	$428: American, Continental, Delta, Northwest, T.W.A., United, USAir	$550: T.W.A.
Boston-Dallas/Fort Worth	$306: Delta	$1,284: Delta
Chicago-Los Angeles	$324: America West, American, Delta, Midway, Southwest, United	$438: Southwest
Los Angeles-Seattle	$288: America West	$498: America West
Philadelphia-New Orleans	$179: Delta, USAir	$820: Delta
Washington-Orlando	$288: Delta, Northwest, United, USAir	$780: Delta, Northwest, United, USAir
INTERNATIONAL ROUTES / Dec. 8-14		
New York-Cairo	$1,092: Egyptair, T.W.A.	$2,166: Egyptair, T.W.A.
New York-Frankfurt	$498: Continental, Delta, Lufthansa, T.W.A.	$1,063: Delta, Lufthansa
New York-London	$358: Continental; $359: Virgin Atlantic	$598: Virgin Atlantic
New York-Panama City	$578: American, Pan Am	$920: American, Equatoriana, Pan Am
New York-Toronto	$129: Air Canada, American	$304: Air Canada, American
Chicago-Paris	$464: T.W.A.	$2,336: American, T.W.A., United
Los Angeles-Bangkok	$840: Thai, United	$2,270: Thai, United
Los Angeles-Sydney	$998: Continental, Northwest, United	$2,798: American, Continental, New Zealand, Northwest Qantas, United
Miami-Managua	$320: Aeronica	$390: Aeronica
San Francisco-Montreal	$379: Air Canada, American	$868: American

Fares are for regularly scheduled nonstop and direct flights (no change of plane), including regularly scheduled service by charter airlines. Departure taxes and fuel surcharges are not included. Advance purchase (usually 21 days for domestic flights; 30 days, international), midweek departure, length of stay and other restrictions may apply to discount fares, which are generally nonrefundable. Fares subject to change or cancellation without notice.

Sources: Official Airline Guides Electronic Edition Travel Service, Eaasy Sabre Personal Reservation System and airlines

World Weather in November

City	Average High/Low	P.M. Hum.	Wet Days	City	Average High/Low	P.M. Hum.	Wet Days
Athens	66/53	61	12	Los Angeles	73/50	38	3
Beijing	48/28	NA	3	Madrid	55/42	65	9
Bermuda	74/63	70	13	Mexico City	68/46	41	6
Boston	49/35	65	10	Miami	77/66	64	10
Budapest	47/38	76	14	Moscow	35/26	79	15
Buenos Aires	76/56	60	9	New York	51/37	60	9
Cairo	78/58	38	1	Paris	50/40	79	15
Chicago	47/34	65	10	Phoenix	75/45	38	3
Delhi	84/52	31	0	Rio de Janeiro	79/68	72	13
Dublin	51/39	NA	12	Rome	61/49	66	11
Frankfurt	47/38	77	16	San Francisco	63/51	60	7
Geneva	47/37	76	11	San Juan	84/73	76	19
Hong Kong	74/65	60	2	Stockholm	40/34	85	16
Houston	71/52	58	8	Sydney	74/60	60	12
Jerusalem	70/53	50	4	Tokyo	60/43	58	7
Johannesburg	77/55	45	10	Toronto	43/31	68	13
London	50/42	78	15	Washington	55/38	51	9

Source: The Times Books World Weather Guide

The New York Times Weather Watch offers hourly readings and three-day forecasts for 600 United States and foreign cities. Touch-tone telephones only: 1-900-884-CAST (75 cents a minute).

$1 Equals . . .

Rates paid to individual travelers in the United States for each dollar changed, minus service fees. Rates may be more favorable abroad, or for large businesses.

	Nov. 4, 1991	Year Ago
AFRICA		
Kenya (shilling)*	22.25	18.69
Morocco (dirham)*	8.31	7.79
Senegal (C.F.A. franc)	262.00	234.00
South Africa (rand)*	2.80	2.32
THE AMERICAS		
Argentina (austral)	8,929.00	4,975.00
Brazil (cruzeiro)	795.00	83.44
Canada (dollar)	1.05	1.10
Mexico (peso)	2,924.00	2,695.00
ASIA PACIFIC		
Australia (dollar)	1.19	1.19
Hong Kong (dollar)	7.21	7.24
India (rupee)*	25.96	16.39
Japan (yen)	124.00	120.00
New Zealand (dollar)	1.64	1.52
EUROPE		
Austria (schilling)	10.65	9.72
Belgium (franc)	31.20	28.45
Britain (pound)	0.54	0.48
Denmark (krone)	5.90	5.32
France (franc)	5.35	4.66
Germany (mark)	1.57	1.40
Greece (drachma)*	168.00	139.00
Ireland (punt)	.58	.52
Italy (lira)	1,176.00	1,045.00
Portugal (escudo)	129.00	121.00
Spain (peseta)	98.00	87.32
Sweden (krona)	5.53	5.18
Switzerland (franc)	1.38	1.18
MIDDLE EAST		
Egypt (pound)*	2.75	2.22
Israel (shekel)	2.11	2.07
Turkey (lira)	4,065.00	2,336.00

*The import of bank notes by nonresidents is restricted or prohibited

Source: Thomas Cook Foreign Exchange

WRITING COMPARISONS EXERCISE 4

Think of two things that you might like to compare. You might compare two automobiles, two vacation places, etc. You may choose whatever subjects you wish to compare. Write an essay in which you compare the two. Indicate the strengths and weaknesses of each, and explain which one you prefer and why.

Make a chart in which you list what is similar and what is different about the items you have chosen.

Below list the comparison words you could use to connect some of these ideas. Then write your essay. Be sure to include a general statement which explains what your purpose is.

Comparison Words	*Item 1*	*Item 2*
________________	________________	________________
________________	________________	________________
________________	________________	________________
________________	________________	________________
________________	________________	________________

WRITING COMPARISONS EXERCISE 5

In chapter 8, you wrote reviews of movies and restaurants. Choose two movies or two restaurants and compare them. Explain which one you prefer and why. Prepare some guide questions for yourself to help you think through the comparison. You can also develop a comparison chart such as the one below.

Areas of comparison	*Movie 1*	*Movie 2*
acting	________________	________________
________________	________________	________________
story	________________	________________
________________	________________	________________
scenery	________________	________________
________________	________________	________________

Home sales

The following are property transactions for March 18 to 22 as reported by the Monroe County clerk's office:

BRIGHTON

ADDRESS	Transfer value
90 Dorking Road	82,000
148 Dorking Road	76,500
53 Lac Kine Dr.	109,000
130 Southland Dr.	80,500
2835 Monroe Ave.	1,301,527

EAST ROCHESTER

ADDRESS	Transfer value
335 Garfield Ave.	16,356

MENDON

ADDRESS	Transfer value
29 Hawks View	213,400

PENFIELD

ADDRESS	Transfer value
11 Woodfield Dr.	226,000
1271 Fairport Nine Mile Road	5,000
1529 Creek St.	137,500
76 Horizon Dr.	18,000
93 Tall Tree Dr.	3,218
1757 Qualtrough Road	153,000
1820 Blossom Road	86,000
1022 Penfield Road	109,500
20 Burrows Dr.	92,000
7 Camberly Place	85,040
31 Camberly Place	74,000
2280 Penfield Road	112,000
2278 Penfield Road	112,000
29 South Village Trail	170,915

PERINTON

ADDRESS	Transfer value
72 Eaglesfield Way	105,000
515 County Line Road	195,000
42 Nelson St.	123,000
4 Sheffield Post	17,025
97 Country Downs Cir.	114,000
54 Rosscommon Cres.	150,000
105 Willingate Road	64,000
21 Hunters Pointe	215,500
42 Little Brook Dr.	89,000
48 Acorn Lane	51,500
52 Little Spring Run	116,500
10 Henley Place	119,900
23 Colonial Cir.	140,000
38 Fairways at Woodcliff	245,000

PITTSFORD

ADDRESS	Transfer value
115 Maywood Ave.	148,000
162 Caversham Woods	215,000
5 State St.	350,000
4 Wandering Trail	158,000

ROCHESTER

ADDRESS	Transfer value
4326-4330 Lake Ave.	86,500
4336-4356 Lake Ave.	189,500
99 Valley St.	75,000
183 Weston Road	68,000
49 Harding Road	66,500
32-34 Wyndham Road	23,306
448 Winchester St.	7,835
78 Winchester St.	54,000
143 Rand St.	59,500
558 Pullman Ave.	24,106
581 Pullman Ave.	58,000
387 Magee Ave.	57,000
111 Bidwell Terr.	47,500
105 Mason St.	49,000
45 Whittier Park	24,000
15 Emanon St.	24,028
1253 Norton St.	33,500
66 Ernst St.	33,000
29 Norran Dr.	47,000
32 Pardee St.	42,000
62 Robin St.	50,900
214 Otis St.	25,000
7 Maltby St.	62,000
57 Ries St.	37,500
76 Harris St.	41,000
976-978 N. Clinton Ave.	17,500
563 Clifford Ave.	20,484
268 Alphonse St.	24,000
1020 Clifford Ave.	12,000
474-478 Portland Ave.	70,125
894 North St.	2,000
777 Clinton Ave. North	25,000
7 Thomas St.	12,152
123 Woodbury St.	21,000
59 Fifth St.	40,000
206 Willmont St.	66,000
194 Springfield Ave.	6,057
80 Lawndale Terr.	54,000
10 Diamond Place	4,800
68 Colbourne Road	31,750
453 Garson Ave.	43,663
1492 East Main St.	38,000
1180 Atlantic Ave.	53,000
7 Mount Pleasant Park	18,270
150 McArdle St.	86,000
99 Hortense St.	14,900
109 Thorndale Terr.	38,000
388 Post Ave.	13,000
494 South Clinton Ave.	30,000
35 Nicholson St.	63,000
34 Canterbury Road	130,000
75 Henrietta St.	38,780
162 Benton St.	45,000
325-327 Laburnum Cres.	90,000
35 Van Bergh Ave.	61,000
394 Carling Road	62,000
102 Middlesex Road	62,900
320 Winton Road North	2,000
122 Maxwell Ave.	62,900
175 Winbourne Road	64,500
181 Gregory Hill Road	83,000
98 Laney Road	67,500

Reprinted with permission of the *Times-Union* and *Democrat and Chronicle*, Rochester, NY (April 3, 1991), 3E.

WRITING COMPARISONS EXERCISE 6

On page 184 is a chart that indicates the sale of houses in Monroe County in upstate New York. Notice that each town or city sold a different number of houses and for different prices. After you examine the chart, answer the guide questions below.

1. Where were these houses sold?
2. Which town sold the most houses?
3. Which town sold the most expensive houses?
4. Which town sold the least expensive houses?
5. Which town sold the fewest houses?
6. How many towns did they list?
7. When were the houses listed in the chart sold?
8. What conclusions can you draw from the information?

Imagine that you and your family are planning to move to Monroe County. Your parents have asked you to do some research about the houses in the area. Using the chart below, write about the housing situation in Monroe County, and make a recommendation for them to consider one of these areas to live in. Explain why you have chosen this area. (Use a separate sheet of paper.)

WRITING COMPARISONS EXERCISE 7

Many people invest in the stock market. Sometimes they make money and sometimes they lose money. On page 186 is a page from *The New York Times* listing some prices for stocks on the New York Stock Exchange.

The list tells you the 52-week high and low in the first column. These are the highest and lowest prices the stock sold for in the past year. In the next column the list gives the names of the stocks and tells what they sold for on that day. It then shows the highest and lowest prices for each stock on that day. The last column shows the amount that the price of the stock has gone up or down since the previous day.

Read the stock listing in a local newspaper, and choose three stocks in which you might like to invest. Decide how much money you would like to invest in each. (Since you are not actually buying the stocks, you can choose whatever amount you want! Just remember that you must complete the mathematics at the end of the week.) Then check the newspaper every day for a week to see how the stock is doing. Use the charts under the heading "My Imaginary Stocks" to record the ups and downs of each of your stocks. When the week is up, proceed to the heading "Guide Questions," and complete the exercise.

New York Stock Exchange Continued

CONSOLIDATED TRADING/WEEK ENDED FRIDAY APRIL 5 1991

52-Week High	52-Week Low	Stock	Div	Yld %	PE Ratio	Sales 100s	High	Low	Last	Chg.
51	42	IlPow pf	4.26	8.4	...	1308	50⅞	49¾	50⅞	+ ¼
39½	31	IlPow pf	3.75e	9.9	...	x24u	39½	37¾	37¾	...
33½	25	IlPow pf	3.00e	9.2	...	x14	33¼	32	32¾	+ 1¼
48½	34	IlPow pf	4.47	9.5	...	z500	47¼	47	47	+ ¼
57¾	39¼	ITW	.72	1.3	16	2448	56¾	53¾	53⅞	− 1¼
110½	48	Imcera	1.00	1.0	30	4277u	110½	95	103½	+ 4⅛
49½	39	Imcer pf	4.00	8.7	...	3	46	45	46	+ ½
18⅛	6⅝	Imoind	.50	3.0	14	2392	17⅝	15⅞	16¾	...
85¼	59¾	ICI	5.48e	7.4	11	1365	75⅝	72⅞	73⅞	+ ¾
34⅝	22¾	INCO	1.00	2.9	8	16198u	34⅝	33	34	+ ⅝
18¼	10½	India	.16e	1.2	...	440	13½	13	13¼	...
80⅞	71	IndiM pf	7.08	9.1	...	z3930	77½	76½	77½	+ 2
87	76½	IndiM pf	7.76	9.2	...	z60	84	84	84	− 1
25	21⅜	IndiM pf	2.15	8.8	...	51	24½	23¾	24½	+ ⅝
26	22½	IndiM pf	2.25	9.0	...	18	25¼	25	25⅛	− ⅛
25½	18¾	IndiEn	1.36	5.6	15	518	24¾	23⅞	24½	− ⅛
16½	8⅞	Indon n	.72e	7.1	...	344	10⅞	10⅛	10⅛	− ⅝
60½	28½	IngerRd	1.32	3.0	13	7422	47⅜	44¼	44½	− 1⅞
35⅞	18⅞	InldStl	.60	3.1	...	5278	20⅞	19	19¼	− 1⅝
50	47	IldSt pfG		...	...	621	49⅝d	47	47	− 2⅝
6⅛	2½	InspRs		...	...	3380	3½	3⅛	3⅜	+ ⅛
⅝	3/64	Integra		...	...	446	3/16	⅛	11/64	+ 1/64
3/16	1/32	Integ pf		...	...	285	7/64	5/64	7/64	− 1/64
16½	6⅛	Intelcal		...	9	6777	11½	9⅜	10	+ ⅛
1¾	½	Intlog		...	...	883	1⅛	1	1	− ⅛
9⅝	4⅞	IntRFn		...	56	648u	9⅝	8¼	9	+ ¾
15¼	15	Intcapln n		...	...	109	15¼	15⅛	15⅛	− ⅛
21¼	16¾	ItcpSe	1.98	10.2	...	x266	19¾	19⅛	19½	...
13/16	1/16	viInterc		...	...	2297	13/32	5/16	11/32	− 1/32
14	2¾	Intrlke		...	12	732	4¼	3⅝	4⅛	− ⅛
30	18⅞	IntAlu	1.00	3.5	9	145	29⅝	28¾	28⅞	− ¾
139¾	96¼	IBM	4.84	4.3	11	89904	114¾	111⅛	112⅝	− 1¼
87⅜	57	IntFlav	2.40	3.0	20	6223	81⅜	75	81	+ 4¼
30½	9	IGame s		...	22	1868u	30½	27½	29⅞	+ 1⅛
45	27¼	IntMult	1.18a	2.7	19	1404u	45	42¾	44⅜	+ 1¾
65⅛	42¾	IntPap	1.68	2.8	12	18644	61⅝	59⅛	60	− 1
21⅝	10¾	IntlRec		...	18	269	18	17⅝	17⅞	+ ⅛
24¼	4¼	IntRect		...	27	14220u	24¼	19¼	24	+ 4½
12⅛	6⅜	IT Crp		...	21	3749	10⅞	10⅛	10½	− ⅜
46	29¼	IntpbGp	.76	1.7	18	4026	45	43⅞	43⅞	− 1⅜
29⅝	22⅞	IntstPw	2.04	6.9	12	944u	29⅝	28⅜	29⅝	+ 1⅛
27¼	24	InPw pr	2.28	8.8	...	z2620	27	25¼	26	+ ½
41½	15½	Intrtan		...	17	917	25½	23⅛	23⅝	+ ⅜
4⅝	1⅝	IntJhn		...	...	670u	4⅝	3⅞	4½	+ ⅝
46¾	22¼	Ionics		...	40	1205	44¾	40½	43½	+ 3⅛
22	18¾	IowllG s	1.71	8.0	11	1997	21¾	21	21½	+ ⅜
28	23⅛	Ipalco	1.88	6.8	11	1259	28	27⅛	27¾	− ¼
11⅞	6½	IrishIn	.33e	4.0	...	275	8⅜	8	8¼	+ ¼
15¼	9	Italy	1.18e	11.0	...	192	10⅞	10⅝	10¾	− ⅛
22¼	7⅝	Itel		...	...	21893	15⅛	12⅝	14¼	+ ⅞
53⅞	20½	Itel pf	3.37	9.4	...	252	37½	34¼	35¾	+ 1¾
8½	6	JHM LP	1.20e	14.1	10	648	8½	8⅛	8½	+ ⅜
30	12½	JWP s		...	13	9384	20¾	19¾	19⅞	− ⅛
11⅛	6¾	Jackpot	.32b	3.0	18	848	11	10⅛	10½	+ ½
43¾	14⅝	Jacobs s		...	27	1007	38	35½	37⅞	+ 2⅛
14½	6⅛	Jakarta	.14e	1.8	...	288	7¾	7⅝	7¾	...
29¼	18½	JRiver	.60	2.2	58	11167	27¾	26	27⅛	+ ⅛
44¼	32½	JRvr pf	3.37	7.8	...	55	43⅞	42½	43¼	...
45½	34⅛	JRvr pf	3.50	7.9	...	231	44½	43⅜	44½	+ ¾
7¼	1¾	Jamswy		...	...	7296	4⅝	3¼	4½	+ ⅞
16¾	7⅛	JpOTC	.70e	5.7	...	3718	12⅞	11¾	12¼	+ ⅜
44¾	32½	JeffPl	1.52	3.4	10	2179	44⅝	42⅞	44⅜	+ 1¼
47½	39½	JerC pf	4.00	8.8	...	z10	45½	45½	45½	− ½
91½	82	JerC pf	8.12	9.1	...	z40	89⅛	89⅛	89⅛	− ⅛
88½	79¼	JerC pf	7.88	8.9	...	z17100	88⅛	88⅛	88⅛	...
24¾	22⅛	JerC pf	2.18	8.9	...	12	24⅝	24⅜	24⅝	...
99½	55½	JohnJn	1.36	1.5	27	40375	97¼	93⅛	93⅜	− 2½
31⅞	17⅛	JohnCn	1.24	4.5	14	3111	28⅛	27⅜	27⅝	− ½
9¼	6⅜	Johnln	.12e	1.4	45	23	8⅝	8⅛	8½	+ ½
38⅝	23⅜	Josten	.80	2.1	24	4010u	38⅝	37	37¼	...
19½	11	KLM	1.02e	7.0	...	1635	14¾	13⅞	14½	+ ½
43½	23⅜	K mart	1.72	4.2	11	20856	42⅝	40⅛	40⅝	− ⅜
26½	20⅞	KN Eng	1.12	5.0	12	519	23⅛	22	22¼	− ⅝
18¾	13¾	KanPip	2.20	12.2	...	221	18½	18	18	− ½
6¼	3⅛	Kaneb		...	...	5296	5¼	4¾	5	...
8¾	7⅝	Kanb pf	.54e	7.0	...	26	7⅞	7¾	7¾	− ⅛
36⅜	29⅛	KCtyPL	2.68	7.5	12	5324	36	35⅜	35⅞	...
45½	39	KCPL pf	3.80	8.5	...	z310	44½	43¾	44½	+ 3
52	46½	KCPL pf	4.50	8.7	...	z100u	52	51	52	+ 2
27	22¾	KCPL pf	2.20	8.3	...	17	26½	25¾	26½	+ ½
27¼	24	KCPL pf	2.33	8.7	...	20	26¾	26	26¾	+ ⅝
50¾	33½	KCSou	1.08	2.4	11	1086	45¾	43⅛	45¼	+ 2
16	12	KCSo pf	1.00	7.4	...	z210	13½	12¾	13½	+ ¼
27¾	19⅝	KanGE	1.72	6.2	14	1526	27¾	27¼	27⅝	...
24⅞	19¾	KansPL	1.86	7.7	11	3879u	24⅞	23¾	24¼	+ ⅜
27¾	14¾	Katyln	.06e	.3	5	570	20¼	19⅝	19¾	...
15¼	5⅜	KaufBH	.30	2.0	16	12153u	15¼	13⅞	15	+ ¾
95½	60⅛	Kellogg	2.12	2.3	22	8235u	95½	91⅝	93¼	− ⅛
17¼	5¼	Kellwd	.80	5.6	49	2738	14⅜	14	14¼	...
43⅛	17⅛	Kemper	.92	2.6	144	3720	37½	33¼	36	+ 2½
9⅛	5	KmpHi	1.05	13.5	...	1656	8	7¾	7¾	− ⅛
10	7⅝	KmplGv	.88	9.5	...	3141	9¼	9	9¼	+ ⅛
10¼	6⅞	KmpMl	1.26	13.8	...	1557	9¼	8¾	9⅛	+ ⅜
12	10⅜	KmpMu	.87	7.3	...	1541	11⅞	11⅝	11⅞	+ ⅛
12⅛	10⅛	KmpStr	.90	7.6	...	625	11⅞	11⅝	11⅞	+ ¼
37⅝	24¼	Kenmt	1.16	3.2	12	778	37	35⅞	36⅝	+ ⅞
20	8⅛	KentEl		...	22	1172u	20	16¾	20	+ 2⅛
22⅛	17¼	KyUtil	1.50	6.8	11	1993u	22⅛	21⅛	22⅛	+ ⅞
11½	4⅜	KerrGl	.33j	...	...	202	7⅛	6¼	7⅛	+ ¾
20⅜	11⅞	KerG pf	1.70	11.1	...	9	15⅜	14¾	15⅜	+ ½
53⅝	41	KerrMc	1.44	3.5	18	6087	43½d	41	41¼	− 1⅝
33	16⅞	Keycp	1.36	4.2	9	6781u	33	30½	32⅝	+ 2
25¾	10	KeyCo s		...	8	251	11½	10	11½	+ 1⅜
15½	9½	MGMG		...	...	1048	15⅜	13⅝	14⅛	+ ⅜
⅞	5/16	MHI Gp		...	20	1104	19/32	½	19/32	+ 3/32
18¼	1⅞	MNC		...	...	6072	4⅝	4¼	4⅜	− ⅛
15	6¾	Magntk		...	10	4251u	15	13½	14¾	+ ⅞
2½	5/64	Major		...	...	28	½	7/16	7/16	...
18	9⅞	Malaysa	.21e	1.5	...	432	14⅝	13⅞	14	− ⅝
7¼	5½	ManhNt		...	102	26	6¼	6	6⅛	+ ⅛
22⅝	10¼	ManrCr	.13	.6	30	5568u	22⅝	20	22¼	+ 1⅜
15⅝	9⅛	Manpwr		...	...	4838	13½	12⅜	13	+ ½
38¼	15	MfrHan	1.88	7.2	21	14898	27⅜	24½	26⅛	+ ½
42	27¾	MfrH pf	4.73e	12.4	...	338	39⅛	37	38⅛	+ ½
38	22⅛	MfrH pf	4.22e	11.8	...	586	35⅞	34½	35¾	+ ⅞
25	17⅝	MfrH pf	2.74	11.2	...	591	24½	24	24⅜	+ ⅛
8½	4	Manvlle		...	7	1966	5¾	5½	5½	− ⅛
11¼	7⅝	Manvl pf		...	...	170	10⅞	10⅝	10⅝	...
2⅝	9/16	Manvl wt		...	...	153	1¼	1⅛	1⅛	...
50	37	MAPCO	1.00	2.0	12	3567u	50	48⅛	49½	+ ¾
1½	⅜	Marcde		...	28	1213	9/16	½	9/16	− 1/16
30¾	22⅝	MarM pf	3.37e	11.7	...	11	29	28¾	28¾	...
39⅝	22¾	MarMD	.80	2.1	22	12117	38¾	37⅞	38½	+ ⅝
8⅝	5⅜	Maritrn	1.15	15.3	9	423	7⅝	7⅛	7½	+ ¼
14	6⅝	MrkIV s	.10b	.9	7	1453	11⅜	10⅝	11⅛	− ⅛
27⅜	8⅜	Marriot	.28	1.5	39	17354	18⅝	17	18⅛	+ 1
87¼	59¾	MrshMc	2.60	3.1	20	x7248u	87¼	83½	84⅛	− 1
30¼	17	Mrshln		...	11	604	25½	24½	24⅝	− ⅞
18	5½	Martch		...	19	2940	15⅛	12⅞	14¼	− ¾
8½	1⅞	MartnL		...	5	1425	2⅝	2⅛	2⅛	− ⅜
59½	34¼	MartM	1.50	2.7	8	9073	57¼	54⅞	55	− 1¼
26¾	14¼	Masco	.56	2.5	25	15724	23⅜	22½	22¾	− ¼
25⅜	17¼	MasCp	2.80	11.5	...	138	24¼	23⅝	24¼	+ ¼
8¼	6⅛	MasPrt	.88	11.0	...	575	8	7⅝	8	+ ¼
149⅞	114	Matsu	.52e	.4	17	97	131	123½	128¾	+ 4¾
26⅝	15½	Mattel	.12	.5	14	7490u	26⅝	25	25⅝	...
11	7⅝	MauLoa	1.15e	11.6	26	956	9⅞	9⅜	9⅞	+ ¼
13	7¼	Maxus		...	...	13352	8½	8	8¼	− ⅛
40⅝	34½	Maxus pf	4.00	10.8	...	81	37⅞	37⅛	37⅛	− ⅜
59⅛	37⅜	MayDS	1.62	3.0	14	11360	55¾	52¾	54⅛	+ ⅞
19⅛	9⅞	Maytag	.50	3.5	15	16575	15¼	14⅛	14¼	− 1
23½	13¼	McClat	.20	.9	23	847	22⅛	20¼	21⅜	+ 1
35½	26⅛	McDr pf	2.20	7.3	...	91	30	28½	30	+ 1¾
26⅞	24⅜	McDr pf	2.60	9.7	...	15	26¾	26¼	26¾	...
34½	20½	McDerl	1.00	3.8	...	7475	26⅜	24⅜	26⅜	+ 1¾
8⅝	4⅛	McDld	.20	2.3	45	545u	8⅝	7⅛	8⅝	+ 1½
38½	25	McDonl	.34	1.0	16	47105	36	33⅞	35¾	+ 1
57½	26½	McDnD	1.40	3.4	5	12310	42	37⅜	41⅛	+ 3⅝
62¾	39⅞	McGrH	2.20	3.5	18	8097u	62¾	58¾	62¼	+ 3¾
38	26⅞	McKes	1.60	4.9	15	3330	33¼	32¼	32⅜	− ½
120	88	McK pf	1.80	1.7	...	1	106	106	106	+ 1
34¼	19½	Mead	1.00	3.4	65	4005	30¼	29¼	29⅜	− ⅞
24⅝	15⅛	Mesrx	.44	2.0	20	2665	23	21¾	21⅞	− 1⅛
23⅜	16¼	Meditr	2.33	10.2	15	2444u	23⅜	22⅛	22⅞	+ ⅝
122	61	Medtrn	.82	.7	28	x4782u	122	117¼	118⅝	− ⅛
19⅜	11	Medusa		...	12	466	16½	15½	16½	+ ½
30	17⅝	Mellon	1.40	5.1	10	5560	28	26¼	27⅝	+ 1⅜
28	25	Mellon pf	2.80	10.3	...	105	27⅞	27	27⅛	− ¼
19⅜	15½	Mellon pf	1.69	9.2	...	120	18½	17¾	18⅜	...
27⅛	23	Melon pfH	2.60	9.6	...	423	27⅛	26⅜	27	+ ⅜
57¾	32¾	Melvile	1.44	2.8	14	12101	53¼	50¾	51⅞	− 1
45⅜	24¼	MercSt	1.02	2.6	11	2241	40¼	38	38⅝	− ⅜
109¾	68¾	Merck	2.24	2.1	23	26811u	109¾	104⅝	106¾	+ 1¼
24⅜	10¾	MerFn	.40	1.7	24	1792u	24⅜	22	24	+ 1⅛
32½	20⅝	Merdth	.64	2.3	...	1268	28	26¾	27½	+ ⅛
38½	16⅛	MerLyn	1.00	2.6	24	42788u	38½	34⅝	37¾	+ 2⅞
29¼	8⅝	MeryG		...	25	6232	28¼	26¼	27⅛	− ⅜
6⅜	1⅛	MesaLP		...	...	12242	3	2⅜	2⅞	+ ⅛
7¼	2¼	MesLP pf	.75i	...	...	5897	3½	3	3½	+ ¼
13/16	1/16	MesaOf	.05i	...	2	4103	5/16	¼	¼	− 1/16
47¼	35⅞	MesaR	2.91	8.0	14	12	36½d	35⅞	36¼	− ¼
4⅛	2⅛	Mesab	.25e	9.5	...	1663	2⅞	2⅜	2⅝	− ⅛
11⅛	5⅝	Mestek		...	10	1005u	11⅛	9⅛	11⅛	+ 1¾
44	40	MtE pfC	3.90	9.1	...	z190	42¾	42	42¾	+ ½
88¼	77½	MtE pfG	7.68	9.1	...	z200	84¼	84¼	84¼	− ¾
93½	84⅛	MtE pfJ	8.32	9.3	...	z40	89	89	89	...
91	81½	MtE pfI	8.12	9.2	...	z50	88½	88½	88½	+ ½
92½	84¼	MtE pfH	8.32	9.3	...	z100	89¼	89¼	89¼	− 1¼
16⅛	8½	MetrFn	.50	3.3	5	1570u	16⅛	14½	15⅜	+ ½
24½	16½	MetFn pf	2.00	8.3	...	588u	24½	23	24	+ ¾
11⅞	8⅛	MexEq n	.58e	5.7	...	915	10½	10⅛	10¼	...
17½	11	MexFd	.40e	2.3	...	4587u	17½	16¾	17¼	+ ¼
26½	24	MCGC pf	2.05	8.5	...	2	24¼	24¼	24¼	− ¼
3⅝	1¾	Micklby	.06	2.0	30	221	3	2⅞	3	+ ⅛
18⅛	6¾	MicrTc		...	...	30974u	18⅛	15½	17⅛	+ 1
30⅝	29¾	MAWste		...	...	14630	30⅝	29¾	30⅝	...
13½	2⅛	viMdwAr		...	...	7389	4	3¼	3¼	− ⅝
20¾	2¾	viMdA pf	1.41j	...	...	347	5⅜	4¼	4⅜	− ⅝
20	17⅜	MdwRs n	1.56	8.0	16	2411u	20	19¼	19½	...
45⅛	26⅜	Millipre	.44	1.0	43	2218u	45⅛	41¾	42½	+ ⅛
5	2⅝	MlePr n		...	...	44	4¼	3¾	4	− ¼
6¼	3½	MilPr pf		...	...	112	5⅜	4⅞	5	− ½
93¾	73⅝	MMM	3.12	3.5	15	18256	90⅝	87½	88⅝	+ ⅛
28¾	22¼	MinnPL	1.90	6.8	12	499	27⅞	27	27¾	+ ½
2½	13/16	Mitel		...	...	1020	1⅜	1¼	1¼	...
19¼	11⅜	MitsbBk	.06r	.3	...	9	18½	18¼	18½	+ ⅜
69½	55⅛	Mobil	2.90	4.5	14	30555	65⅝	63⅝	64	− ½
24⅝	13⅛	MolBio		...	...	1238	24½	23⅛	23¾	+ ⅜
16¾	⅜	MonCa		...	...	6690	1⅞	1	1½	− ¼
42	1½	MonCa pf	5.00j	...	...	274	12	5	7	− 3½
16¾	8¾	Monrch	.20	1.8	124	841	11⅝	10⅞	11⅛	...
62½	38¾	Monsan s	1.94	3.4	13	14181	59¼	56⅝	56⅝	− 1⅜
22⅞	17⅜	MonPw	1.48	6.7	12	x8324u	22⅞	21¾	22¼	+ ¾
16⅞	10	Monted	.41e	3.2	4	29	12¾	12⅛	12¾	+ ½
18⅝	15	MonSt	1.76	9.6	...	259	18¼	17⅞	18¼	+ ¼
30¼	21	Moore	.94	3.8	20	1609	25⅜	24¾	25	...
49½	29⅝	Morgan	1.98	4.2	12	18564	48½	46⅜	47⅜	+ ⅝
60	55	Morgn pf	5.00e	8.7	...	205	57⅞	57⅛	57⅝	+ ¼
78	71½	OhEd pf	7.24	9.3	...	z990u	78	76½	78	+ ½
80	72½	OhEd pf	7.36	9.4	...	z300	78	77	78	− ¾
25¾	23½	OhEd pf	2.44e	9.6	...	2443	25⅜	25¼	25⅜	− ⅛
87⅜	80¼	OhEd pf	8.20	9.6	...	z480	86	85½	85½	− 1
96	88	OhEd pf	9.12	9.6	...	z420	94⅞	93½	94⅞	+ ⅝
94	85½	OhEd pf	8.64	9.6	...	z80	90	90	90	− 1
88	79	OhP pf	8.04	9.3	...	z440	88	85	86	...
86⅞	77¼	OhP pfB	7.60	8.9	...	z150	85½	85½	85½	+ ⅜
87½	76⅜	OhP pfC	7.60	9.0	...	z300	84¼	84¼	84¼	− ¼
26	24½	OhP pfG	2.27	8.9	...	38	25½	25⅛	25½	+ ¼
95	86½	OhP pfE	8.48	9.0	...	z1040	94	93½	94	+ ⅝
86½	78¼	OhP pfD	7.76	9.0	...	z200	86½	86	86	+ ¾
40½	32⅞	OklaGE	2.58	6.5	12	x5240u	40½	39¼	39½	+ ⅝
15¼	9	OklaG pf	.80	7.3	...	z2120	11¼	10¼	11	+ ⅜
28⅝	17¼	OldRep	.76b	2.7	7	x1186u	28⅝	26	28	+ 1⅝
57⅜	28⅛	Olin	2.20	5.2	11	959	44½	42⅛	42⅜	− 1¾
13¼	6	Omncre	.12	1.0	34	1272	12⅞	12⅛	12⅝	− ⅛
29⅞	16⅛	Omnicm	1.10	3.7	15	6648u	29⅞	28⅝	29⅜	+ ⅜
10½	4	OnLine		...	13	1196	9¾	9	9¼	− ⅛
14⅜	8¼	Oneida s	.48	3.8	16	1016	12¾	11¾	12½	+ ¼
16⅛	11⅞	ONEOK	.84	6.2	10	2059	13⅝	12⅞	13½	+ ⅝
19¼	11	OpnhCa	1.70a	9.0	11	1398	19¼	18	18⅞	+ ⅝
9	7½	OpMG	.99	11.5	...	x432	8⅞	8⅝	8⅝	...
10⅛	8⅞	OppMS	1.16	11.5	...	3399	10⅛	9⅞	10⅛	+ ⅛
8⅜	4⅜	OrngCo		...	...	197	5⅝	5⅛	5⅛	− ½
33⅜	26⅛	OranRk	2.34	7.0	11	377u	33⅜	32⅝	33⅜	+ ½
32	14⅞	OreStl s	.48	1.6	17	8091	30⅛	28	29¾	+ ¾
4½	2⅛	Orient		...	2	48	3⅛	2¾	2¾	− ¼
24½	13	OrionC	.92	3.8	9	1138u	24½	23	24	+ ⅞
22	13¾	OrionC pf	2.12	9.8	...	178u	22	21⅛	21⅝	+ ¼
36¾	32	OriC pf	4.48e	12.2	...	6	36¾	36¾	36¾	...
26¼	16½	OriC pf	1.90	7.3	...	80u	26¼	24½	26	+ 1
21⅝	6⅞	OrionP		...	...	4451	10¾	9⅝	9¾	− ½
54⅞	31⅛	Oryx	1.20	3.7	14	11892	34⅝	32	32⅛	− 2⅜
24⅝	9	OutbdM	.40	2.4	...	2655	17⅛	16	16¾	+ ¼
26	12½	OvShip	.50	2.6	14	632	19⅜	18⅞	19⅛	...
20	10⅞	OwenM	.26	1.4	19	600	19⅞	18⅞	19¼	− ⅛
26½	13⅝	OwenC		...	13	6345	25⅛	23¾	24	− ½
11	6½	Oxford	.50	4.8	21	105	10⅝	9¾	10½	+ ⅝
37⅛	17⅝	PHH	1.20	4.2	14	x1197	29¼	27½	28⅞	+ 1
15¾	6	PHM	.12	.8	12	1899	14⅞	13¾	14⅝	+ ⅛
40¼	15¾	PNC	2.12	6.9	42	7898	33½	30	30⅝	− 2½
33⅛	14¾	PNC pfC	1.60	6.2	...	4	27	26	26	− 1
33¼	15½	PNC pfD	1.80	7.2	...	11	27½	25	25	− 2
28½	24¾	PNC pfE	2.60	9.5	...	7	27½	26¾	27½	+ 1¼
55¼	34½	PPG	1.68	3.5	11	6770	49½	47⅝	48⅜	− ½
57¼	29⅜	PS Grp	.60	1.1	...	642u	57¼	52⅜	56⅜	+ 3⅜
18¼	14½	PSI	.88	5.0	8	58761	18⅛	17½	17⅝	− ¼
12⅞	10½	PSI pfB	1.04	8.5	...	z1200	12¼	11½	12¼	+ ¼
12¼	11	PSI pfC	1.08	9.4	...	z620	12	11¼	11½	+ ¼
15	12	PacAS	1.46	10.2	...	120	14¾	14⅛	14⅜	− ¼
46⅛	32¾	PacEnt	3.48	9.7	...	4255	36¼	35¼	36	− ⅛
26½	20	PacGE	1.64	6.2	13	22050u	26½	25⅜	26⅜	+ ¼
16⅜	7¼	PacSci		...	50	615	10⅛	9½	10	+ ¼
47⅞	36¼	PacTel	2.14	5.2	16	x21020	43¼	41¼	41½	− ⅞
23½	17½	Pacific	1.44	6.5	12	14774	22¾	21⅞	22¼	+ ¼
24⅝	11	PainWb	.52	2.2	31	8754u	24⅝	22⅛	24	+ 1¼
17¼	11¼	PainW pf	1.37	8.2	...	868u	17¼	16	16¾	+ ½
3	¼	viPAA		...	...	10432	1⅛	1	1⅛	+ ⅛
28½	9⅞	PanEC	.80	5.6	...	7480	14¾	14	14¼	− ⅜
16½	7	Pansph	.20	1.8	10	2520	12⅛	11¼	11¼	− ½
8⅛	3⅜	ParPh		...	...	960	4¾	4⅜	4½	− ¼
5⅞	2⅜	ParTch		...	...	44	4¼	4⅛	4¼	− ¼
50¼	31½	ParCom	.70	1.8	20	26879	41½	38¼	38½	− 2
15⅝	10	ParkEl	.32	2.9	17	47	11⅜	11	11	− ¼
11⅞	5¾	ParkDrl		.1	...	9124	7¾	6⅝	6⅞	− ⅞
32¾	18⅝	ParkHn	.92	3.7	11	4662	25⅜	24½	24¾	− ½
5¼	2¼	PathCm		...	...	631	3⅛	2⅝	2⅞	− ⅜
5⅛	2⅛	PatPtr		...	...	1222	2⅝	2⅜	2⅜	− ¼
10⅞	7	PatrPr	.80	9.3	...	1314	8¾	8⅜	8⅝	+ ¼
11⅜	7⅞	PatPrII n	.90	9.2	...	1002	9⅞	9⅝	9¾	...
15	12⅝	PatSel n	1.65	11.4	...	1260	14½	14	14½	+ ¼
1⅞	⅜	Patten		...	...	616	15/16	¾	⅞	− 1/16
25⅛	15⅜	PenCn	.68	2.9	15	x2642	24¾	23¾	23¾	− ¼
70⅛	37⅜	Penney	2.64	5.0	11	x14500	56¾	52⅜	52⅝	− ¼
46⅛	39	PaPL	3.10	6.9	11	1860u	46⅛	44	45¼	+ ½
52	46½	PaPL pf	4.40	8.6	...	z1260	52	50¼	51	+ ¼
56	47	PaPL pf	4.50	8.7	...	z1770	52	50	51¾	+ 1¼
98½	88	PaPL pf	8.60	8.9	...	z820u	98½	96½	97	...
96¼	86	PaPL pr	8.40	8.9	...	z840	96	94	94½	− ½
104	98¼	PaPL pf	9.24	9.1	...	z400u	104	102	102	+ ½
91⅞	82	PaPL pr	8.00	9.0	...	z880	90½	88	89	− ½
98	88½	PaPL pr	8.70	8.9	...	z1090	98	96	97½	+ 1½
85¼	61¾	Pennzol	3.00	4.2	30	3985	75⅛	71	72⅛	− 3⅛
25¼	20	PeopEn	1.72	7.5	13	1994	24	22⅞	23	− ⅞
17¼	8⅜	PepBoy	.13	1.1	18	18299	12¾	10⅝	12⅛	+ 1¼
35⅝	20½	PepsiC s	.40	1.2	24	112286u	35⅝	32¾	33¼	− 1
16⅛	11¼	PerkF	1.20	8.0	11	523	15½	15	15	− ⅛
31⅜	18⅝	PerkEl	.68	2.6	20	7741	27⅛	26	26¼	− ⅞
5⅞	3¾	Prmian	.60e	15.5	...	1262	4	3¾	3⅞	...
9⅞	3¾	PeryDr		...	...	645	6½	6	6⅛	...
18⅝	15⅛	Pet		...	...	73647	18⅝d	15⅛	15⅞	...
27⅝	12½	Petrie	.20	1.0	331	2614	20⅞	19¼	19⅞	+ ⅜
34	24¼	PetRs	2.35e	8.9	...	512	26⅞	26¼	26½	− ⅜
19⅜	16¼	PetRs pf	1.57	8.8	...	73	17⅞	17½	17⅞	+ ⅛
58⅜	27½	Pfizer s	1.32	2.3	24	43948u	58⅜	53½	56¾	+ 2¾
71⅝	46⅛	PhelpD	3.00	4.8	5	7638	67½	62¾	62⅞	− 4¼
20	14½	PhilaEl	1.20	6.0	[illegible]	15866u	20	19½	19⅞	+ ⅛
42	35½	PhE pfA	3.80	9.4	...	z150	40¼	40¼	40¼	+ ¼
47½	40	PhE pfB	4.30	9.2	...	z10	46¾	46¾	46¾	− ¾
49½	41	PhE pfC	4.40	9.4	...	z10	47	47	47	− 1
50½	43	PhE pfD	4.68	9.4	...	z320	50	49	49¾	− ¼
93¼	81½	PhE pfG	8.75	9.4	...	z1060u	93¼	92	92⅝	+ ⅝
102¾	93¼	PhE pfS	9.50	9.2	...	z10000	102¾	102¾	102¾	...

My Imaginary Stocks

Name of stock #1 ______________________________

The amount of money I invested ______________________

The cost of each share ___________________________

The number of shares ____________________________

Date	*Price*	*Change*

Name of stock #2 ______________________________

The amount of money I invested ______________________

The cost of each share ___________________________

The number of shares ____________________________

Date	*Price*	*Change*

Name of stock #3 ____________________

The amount of money I invested ____________________

The cost of each share ____________________

The number of shares ____________________

Date ***Price*** ***Change***

____

____

____

____

____

____

____

Guide Questions

1. Which stock do you wish you had bought?

____

2. How much money did you invest in all stocks combined?

____

3. How much money did you invest in each stock?

____

4. How did you decide which stocks to invest in?

____

5. Did you make money or lose money during the course of the week?

____

6. On what dates did you purchase each stock?

____

7. How much was each stock worth on those days?

___

8. How much was each stock worth five days later?

___

9. How did each of your stocks do?

___

Now write a short essay on a separate sheet of paper in which you describe what you did and in which you compare how your stocks did. Think about the questions you answered above. Which of them would you use as support for an introduction? Will you talk about the best stock first or last? Where will you discuss the total amount of money you made or lost—in your introduction, in your conclusion, or in both?

Chapter 11

Creating a Class Magazine

In the previous ten chapters, you have written descriptions, parodies, movie, television and restaurant reviews, and instructions for making things. You have talked about travel and the stock market. Essentially, you have done the kind of writing found in magazines.

In this chapter, we will take the work that you have done and use it to create a class magazine!

Before we begin, examine some magazines. Your teacher may provide you with some or ask you to bring some to class. There are many different kinds of magazines. There are magazines about news, computers, nature, sports, fashion, and finance, to mention a few categories. There are also magazines that offer a variety of articles on different subjects: some news, fashion, interviews, sports, cartoons, theatre, etc., all in one magazine. What magazines are you familiar with? What articles do you like to read in magazines?

Just as there are many different types of articles in a magazine, there are also different groups of people who are responsible for those articles. Look at the editorial page of a magazine. There you will see the names and titles of the people who are responsible for producing the magazine. You may see some of the following titles: editor-in-chief, editor, staff writers, art editor, photographers, contributors, reporters, feature writers, and so on.

Since in this class you have written on many different topics, you will produce a general magazine of interest and students will serve as the various editors, writers, photographers, and artists. To do this you will select editors for each of the subject areas your magazine will include. Then you will add groups to work on editing and the actual production of the magazine.

Step 1

Decide which areas you will include in your magazine. Your list should be determined by the kinds of things you wrote in class. It should also be determined by the talent of the people in the class. For example, if you have some talented artists in the class, you might want to form an art department to add visual material to the magazine in the form of cartoons, drawings, or designs. The art department could also be asked to select the sketches students drew to illustrate some of their essays.

If you have some people who are interested in photography, they could be asked to take photographs to go along with the articles. They or the editorial department could then write the captions.

How many departments you have, of course, also depends on how many students there are in your class. Here is a list of some categories which you can use as a guide.

Possible Categories

- reviews

  movies
  television shows
  restaurants

- literature

  stories
  parodies

- business

  stock market information

- travel

- instructions

  how to make things
  recipes
  scientific explanations

- description

  fashion
  events

- interviews
- letters
- features
- advertisements
- art

In addition, you will need an editor-in-chief who will be responsible for seeing to it that everyone does his or her assignment and that the magazine project is successfully completed. The editor-in-chief will need an editorial staff to help determine the size of the magazine (the number and size of the pages), to write headlines or titles for each of the articles, to work with each of the groups, to establish deadlines, and to see to it that they are met and to be sure that there are essays included in the magazine from many different students.

The editorial staff will also determine how the paper will be produced and who will do it. For example, will it be typed, put on a computer, handwritten, photocopied, pasted in a scrapbook?

In addition, the editorial staff will determine how the magazine will be distributed and whether it will go to others outside of the class.

Step 2

Once the list of areas for your magazine has been developed, students will select or be assigned to work in one or, possibly, more areas.

Step 3

Groups should meet to choose an editor for their group. This person will act as the chairperson of the group. The chair's responsibilities are to see to it that the committee or department gets its work done and to encourage the group to generate and share ideas.

Step 4

Each student will go through all of the papers he or she has written in this class and choose five papers that could be used in the magazine.

Step 5

Many of the articles that you will be reading were written at the beginning of the term. As a result, there will be things that you would like to change because you know more about writing now. That is a sign that you have learned and can critique your own work. Congratulations!

Choose five of your favorite papers and make whatever changes you feel would make them better papers. Use all the information that you have learned about colorful words, sentence form, and being concise to improve your essays.

Use scissors and cut up your essay if you want to change the order in which you presented information or if you want to add a paragraph or dialogue. Then just paste the paragraphs together in the new order.

Before you submit your essay to the appropriate group, be sure that your name is on each paper so that you can be given credit.

Step 6

Give each paper to the group responsible for that subject. For example, if you have a review of a restaurant, give it to the group responsible for reviews.

Step 7

Each group will collect papers from the students in the class. It is the responsibility of each group to be sure that there are a selection of papers to choose from.

Members of the group must then read through the papers and choose one or two to include in the class magazine. One way to do this is for the chairperson to give copies of the papers to committee members and to ask them to rank order the papers indicating which paper they like best. Members should also be asked to indicate why they prefer one paper over another. Then the group can meet to try to reach a consensus.

Once the papers to be used have been selected, it is the responsibility of the group to check them and correct any errors. The group may also determine a title or headline for each article they intend to use, but the final decision rests with the editorial department.

The group will then submit its selection of papers to the editorial department.

Step 8

It is up to the editorial department to decide the layout of the magazine. Which articles will go first? What will the cover look like? Will there be a table of contents and who will do it? How will the magazine be reproduced? Will it be typed, entered on a word processor, photocopied, handwritten, or pasted in a scrapbook? What the final magazine looks like will depend on the resources available and the decisions of the editorial department.

Are there people in the class who can draw well? Perhaps they can design the cover and contribute artwork to the interior of the magazine.

The editorial department must determine how many copies are needed and how they will be distributed.

At this point, most of the work of the other departments has been completed, so the editorial department can now ask members of the class to help with the production of the magazine: typing, copying, collating, stapling, etc.

The editorial department may also want to ask the class for suggestions to name the magazine.

The editorial department will want to be sure that the author's name appears with each article. Also, give credit to all the people who worked on the magazine and their title, whether they are reporter, editor, writer, stapler—whatever work each person has done should be recognized.